This Book Is A Gift

From   Apollo-North Apollo

Elementary School P.T.A.

**APOLLO MEMORIAL LIBRARY
APOLLO, PA.**

WITHDRAWN

Close Encounters

CLOSE ENCOUNTERS
A Factual Report on UFOs

by
Sherman J. Larsen

Foreword by J. Allen Hynek

Apollo Memorial Library

RAINTREE
Milwaukee • Toronto • Melbourne • London

Copyright © 1978, Raintree Publishers Limited

All rights reserved. No part of this book may be reproduced or utilized in any form or by any means, electronic or mechanical, including photocopying, recording, or by any information storage and retrieval system, without permission in writing from the Publisher. Inquiries should be addressed to Raintree Publishers Limited, 205 West Highland Avenue, Milwaukee, Wisconsin 53203.

Library of Congress Number: 78-2322

3 4 5 6 7 8 9 0 82 81 80 79

Printed and bound in the United States of America.

Library of Congress Cataloging in Publication Data

Larsen, Sherman J.
   Close encounters: A Factual Report on UFOs

  Bibliography: p. 80.
  Includes index.
  1. Flying saucers. I. Title.
TL789.C6575   001.9'42   78-2322
ISBN 0-8172-1200-0

Table of Contents

Foreword		**6**
Introduction		**8**
Chapter 1	**The UFO Phenomenon**	**10**
Chapter 2	**What Is a UFO?**	**14**
Chapter 3	**A Short History of UFOs**	**20**
Chapter 4	**What Do People Report?**	**28**
Chapter 5	**What Do People See?**	**36**
Chapter 6	**How Do Researchers Study a UFO Report?**	**44**
Chapter 7	**Some UFO Cases**	**50**
Chapter 8	**If You See a UFO**	**62**
Chapter 9	**Conclusion**	**68**
Glossary		**75**
Appendix		**82**
Index		**92**

Foreword

Interest in space, in life elsewhere in the universe, and in UFOs is very great among young people. But getting information is a problem. A lot of good information on astronomy or space matters is easily available. But on UFOs, there is a flood of misinformation — especially in junk newsstand material. It is not possible for the student to tell the good information from the bad.

In this little book, Mr. Larsen has given us a plain-spoken, no-nonsense, factual treatment of the UFO subject. It is especially for younger readers. It is just the guide that has been needed.

The UFO phenomenon is truly a phenomenon of our times. It is made up of many, many events that are reported as UFOs. These reports may be made by people who think the object they saw was unidentified. But most reports become "identified" after examination by a UFO investigator. That does not mean that there are no genuine UFOs. There are. Real UFOs, however, are much rarer than one would think from reading the popular "literature" on UFOs. There we find airplanes, balloons, kites, clouds, planets, and many other ordinary things. Some of these things are reports by people who *want* to see UFOs. They don't actually see them.

When all these ordinary things are cleared away, however, we are left with events that cannot be explained. Mr. Larsen has described these UFOs in simple terms, and he has given examples of them. His treatment might be said to be oversimplified. But he has done that on purpose. This book is for young people, who do not need all the complexities of the UFO subject.

The idea that "we are not alone" has a strong emotional appeal today. Properly guided, that idea can be an enriching and productive force in young peoples' lives and thoughts. Guided wrongly, it can have the opposite effect.

The proper study of UFOs can be a fine introduction to the scientific method. In the first place, high interest is built into the subject. Following where that interest leads, involves applying elements of astronomy and meteorology. The young researcher must also know something about how the mind perceives things and misperceives things. The researcher must know the tricks the eye can play on the mind.

The author has shown the traps one can fall into in misidentifying everyday things as UFOs. But he has also given a good outline of the real UFO events that are left after all the misidentifying has been taken away.

Mr. Larsen does a much-needed service in contributing this practical guide on the puzzling yet intriguing UFO phenomenon.

        J. Allen Hynek
        Director
        Center for UFO Studies

Introduction

My interest in UFOs spans nearly a quarter of a century. My main concern has never been the reports of people who have seen UFOs. What has interested me are UFO events themselves. I have also been interested in why for so many years it was almost impossible to get UFO information from the government. And I have been puzzled by the reasons of some scientists for trying to explain away these UFO events that just "will not go away."

During the past 12 years, I have been a teacher and a lecturer. I have talked to scientific, military, and civic groups. And I have been involved with the general public and with schools of all levels. It was easy to see that the public was also caught up in their search for facts. For the most part, people had to choose between the doubting scientific statements and the sensational reports in the news. The public usually took the latter as the truth.

When I was asked to write this book about UFOs, my answer was not long in coming. This was my chance to give interested people the results of my personal study and also the research available through my close association with Dr. J. Allen Hynek. Together we founded the Center for UFO Studies, a not-for-profit Illinois corporation.

The statistics in this book come from the computer data bank at the Center. This data bank is called UFOCAT. It contains about 100,000 entries. These entries, which are always being added to, make up the UFO record at the Center.

All statements or details of particular UFO reports are taken from the actual stories of the witnesses.

Conclusions for particular UFO reports are the result of research.

In plain language, you will be presented with the facts as best we know them.

ONE
The UFO Phenomenon

For many years there have been strange events happening in the sky. People have reported seeing flying objects that looked and acted differently from any known things. Over the years, there have been thousands of these reports. Witnesses were puzzled by the objects. And scientists often could not explain them. Such an object came to be called an unidentified flying object (UFO). If an object was later explained, it became an identified flying object (IFO).

Feelings are strong about whether or not UFOs exist. Many people think that UFOs *must* exist, simply because there are so many UFO reports. Others feel that because some objects turned out to be either IFOs or fakes, *all* objects could be explained. But neither group is right. Neither group takes a scientific, thoughtful approach to the UFO problem. Our efforts will be devoted to describing, discussing, and analyzing UFO reports and statistics.

UFOs have been reported from nations of all seven continents. The reports have come from cities, towns, and farm areas. And the reports have come from all kinds of people. But no matter where or who the reports come from, there are certain things that are similar.

Witnesses usually report that the object seems to be a material thing. It moves through the sky in an unusual way. The speed, movement, and shape are different from any known earth craft.

During the day, the object seems to be metal. The colors silver, aluminum, and gray are the most common. The object does not seem to be lit.

At night, the object is lit. Either the whole object glows or there are individual lights. Red, orange, and white are the colors most reported.

Objects have been seen as "blips" on radar screens. In a few rare cases, an object was seen in the sky at the same time and place that it was seen on radar.

There may be rapid increases in speed, abrupt stops, or sharp turns. The object may move up and down or it may hover. In some cases, the object has dived into water and come out again. Sometimes the objects land on the ground. Objects reported to be near the ground or to have landed on the ground often change the earth. An object may dent the ground or burn the foliage. The object may completely change the soil.

Observers have reported that an object did not move away, it just faded away.

Some are reported to have occupants while others do not have occupants.

All this information leads us to the realization that UFOs are really being observed. We call them the UFO phenomenon.

About 900 UFO events are reported to the government, police, or UFO organizations each year. However, each year there are several thousand events that are not reported. There are two main reasons that UFO sightings are not reported. First, many people simply do not know to whom they should make a report. In other cases, people are afraid they might be laughed at.

The white spot in the upper right-hand corner of the photo at the left was reported as a UFO.

The photo at the right is an enlargement of the left photo. It was taken during NATO maneuvers during Operation Mainbrace.

People who do not believe in UFOs have given some of the following reasons. It has been suggested that science fiction movies, TV programs, and the Space Age have caused people to "see" things. This could not be the case. UFOs were reported before we had a space program, TV, or movies. Further, UFO reports usually come in waves, known as "flaps." A flap occurs when there are a number of UFO sightings within a short time period in a small geographical area.

Some people think that UFOs are secret craft of our government or another. This claim also does not hold up under study. UFOs have been studied for more than 30 years. It would be almost impossible to keep something secret for that long. Details of such a craft might not be known, but the craft itself would be. Thousands of people would be involved with such a craft. Parts would have to be manufactured and transported. Then the craft would have to be assembled. With all this work and all these people, how could such a craft stay a secret?

Let's look at some of the opinions people have about UFOs. In 1973 there was a UFO flap. In a Gallup poll following the flap, 11% of those polled said they had seen a UFO. Also, 51% said they believed UFOs were real, not the imagination of those who saw them.

In May 1975, Dr. Peter Sturrock of the Institute for Plasma Physics at Stanford University conducted a survey of the members of the American Astronomical Society. The members of the society are professional astronomers, physicists, and mathematicians. Of the 2,611 members polled 1,356 or 52% responded.

One question was: Do you think that the UFO problem deserves scientific study? Here are the answers: 23% said certainly, 30% said probably, 27% said possibly, 17% said probably does not, and 3% said certainly does not. You can see that most members had a positive attitude. Only 20% expressed a negative attitude. Of the 1,356 who replied, 62 said they had witnessed a UFO or had made some type of instrumental record of a UFO event. A total of 65 events could not be identified.

Finally, a recent Gallup poll in the United States revealed that 96% had heard about "flying saucers." That is one of the highest "public awareness" scores ever recorded by the Gallup organization. The poll also said that 5,000,000 Americans claim to have seen a UFO. Six million people believed that flying saucers were from another planet.

From all this information, the conclusion must be reached that a phenomenon does exist. The UFO phenomenon!

The next question is: What Is a UFO?

TWO
What Is a UFO?

Despite all you have heard and read, there is no conclusive evidence that any government or group has in its possession a UFO or a part of a UFO. (One possible exception is described at the end of Chapter 7.) Also, there is no evidence that anyone possesses an alien being, dead or alive. So, scientists cannot study UFOs. There are none. What scientists *do* study are reports of UFO experiences.

Keeping this in mind, we can properly evaluate our knowledge as we describe and define a UFO.

To an observer, a UFO is simply the experience of seeing something that is unidentifiable because of the strangeness of its shape, movement, or activity. At night the object seems to be a light source. During the day the object seems material.

If the observer passes the details of such an event on to the government or a UFO study group, the event becomes a report.

Scientists or others investigate the report. After

thorough study, if the report cannot be explained, the UFO report becomes a UFO case. About 10% of UFO reports stand up to this study and become UFO cases.

A UFO report may include drawings, photographs, motion pictures, and soil or plant samples. A few reports have included what are supposed to be pieces or parts of UFOs.

The foremost authority of the UFO phenomenon, Dr. J. Allen Hynek, has described and defined UFO experiences. The following explanations are from the definitions in his book called *The UFO Experience*.

All UFO reports may be put into three classes.

Nocturnal Light (NL). An NL is a light or several lights seen at night. The viewer cannot tell how far away the lights are. These lights may be constant, flashing, or rotating. The lights may move steadily, dart about, or hover.

Daylight Disc (DD). A DD seems to be a material object. It is seen during the day. Again, the observer cannot tell how far away the object is. The object may move in one direction, it may change course, it may move rapidly up and down, or it may hover.

Radar-Visual (RV). Blips are seen on a radar screen, at the same time the object is being seen by others. The distance to the object can be determined by the radar.

If the UFO event takes place within about 500 feet of the observer, the report is called a close encounter. Close encounters are divided into three groups.

Close Encounters of the First Kind (CE I). In a CE I, the UFO may be in the sky or near the ground. The observer is close enough to see certain details of the UFO. For example, if you are 500 feet from an automobile, you can tell certain things about it. You could see whether it had four doors or two. You could tell its color. And you could probably tell the brand of car.

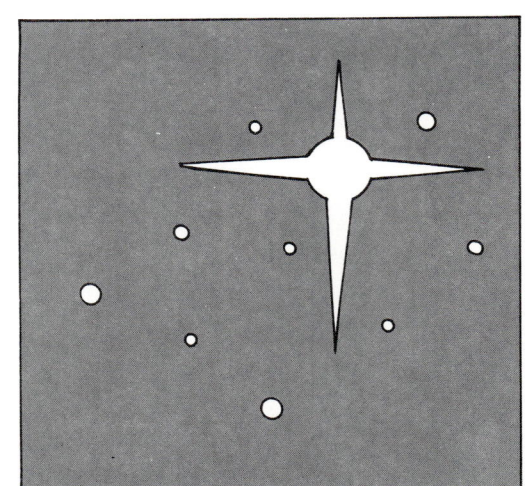

Figure 1
Nocturnal Light
(NL)

Figure 2
Daylight Disc
(DD)

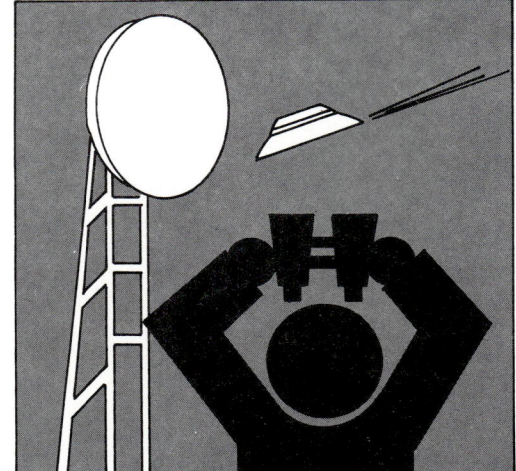

Figure 3
Radar-Visual
(RV)

Figure 4
Close Encounter
of the First Kind
(CE I)

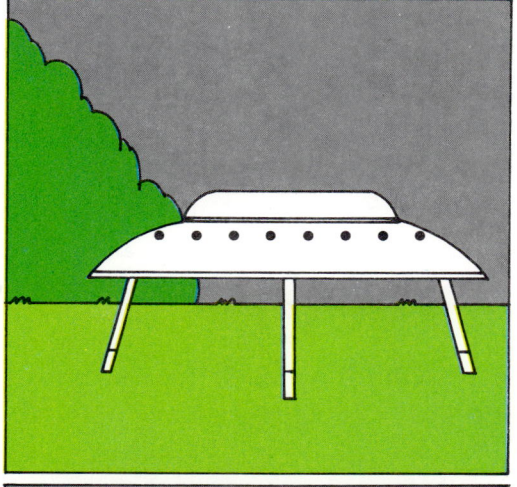

Figure 5
Close Encounter
of the Second Kind
(CE II)

Figure 6
Close Encounter
of the Third Kind
(CE III)

Close Encounters of the Second Kind (CE II). In these reports, the UFO has landed on or is near the ground. The observer may or may not have seen the UFO land. When a UFO lands, some interaction with the surface is often reported. The soil may be dented, or grass may be burned. There may have been a chemical change in the soil. Electrical and communications interference is often reported. For example, cars, telephones, and television sets may not work. Some reports say that animals seemed to be frightened by the landing.

Close Encounters of the Third Kind (CE III). In a CE III, the observer sees what seems to be an occupant in the UFO. The occupant may appear to be a living being or a robot.

In July 1968, hearings on UFOs were held in Congress before the Committee on Science and Astronautics. The chart in Figure 7 was introduced into the hearings. The chart shows the various UFO shapes reported to the Air Force. In general, the shapes represented acceptable shapes from UFO reports. Some, however, were not acceptable.

Among the acceptable UFO shapes are 1A, 6A, 6E, 7A, 7E, and 8F. These were reported from various parts of the United States, France, and South America.

Examples of shapes that were proved to be fakes are 2G, 3G, 6B, 7B, and 8B.

What this chart shows is the similarity of the reported UFO shapes. All examples are basically a disc. The very fact that all reports are all so similar is in itself strange. Wouldn't it be reasonable that there would be many different shapes? But no, the shapes are basically the same. Why? Could it be because there *are* UFOs and they have this basic shape?

Before we discuss what people report and what they see, you should have some historical background.

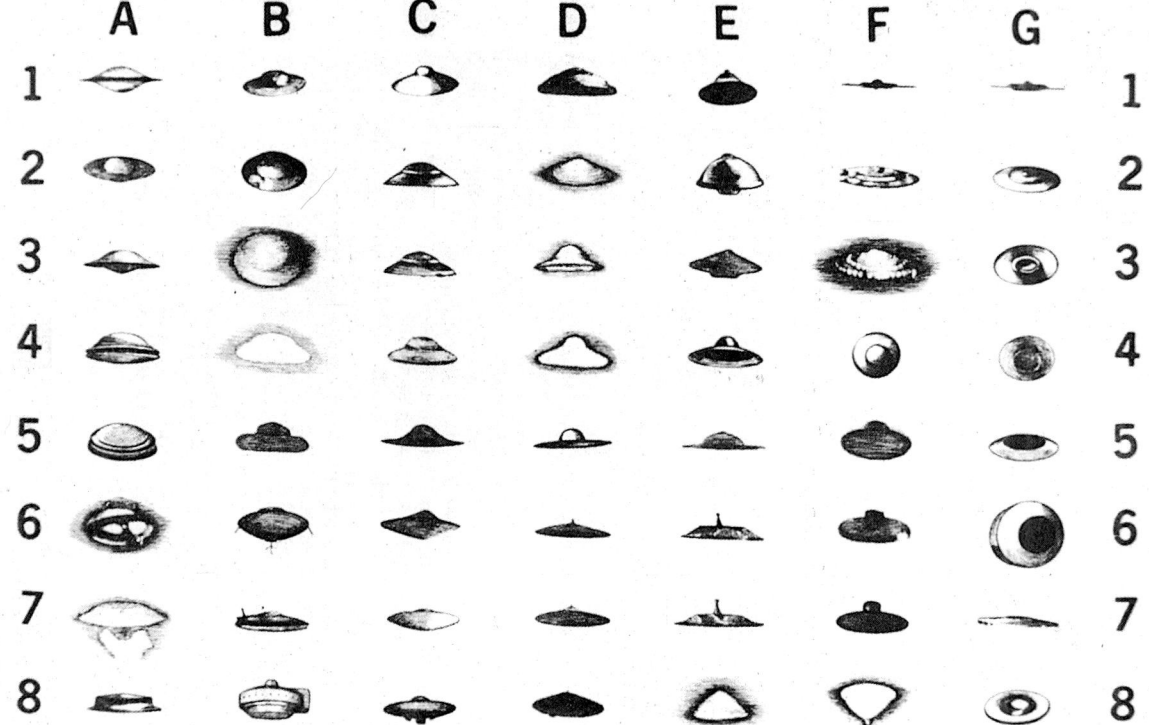

Figure 7 — This chart shows most of the shapes of UFOs reported to the Air Force. To find a particular shape, look across the numbered row. Then look up to find the letter. For example, 6E is the fifth shape over in row 6.

THREE
A Short History of UFOs

The UFO mystery, like so many other mysteries, seems to recur throughout history. Some people think that UFO history goes back to the Stone Age. Ancient cave drawings picture an object shaped like a disc or cigar. Other drawings look something like a person dressed in what seems to be a helmet or space suit. Some people assume these drawings are the first UFO reports. But we cannot even study that assumption. So it is best to pass over these ancient drawings.

Probably the next earliest source offered as a record of UFOs are the writings of the Far East. Things that could be UFOs are mentioned in these writings. As we continue down through history, we find other records that could be interpreted as being about UFOs. Church records are one example. Military records have reported "flaming shields" in the night. Other historical records mention flaming stones falling from the sky. Objects that could be UFOs are mentioned in the Bible.

But the problem with all these writings is always the same. That is, there is no way to prove that any of these "UFO reports" are real. So let us move up to the present. The real history of UFOs begins in 1947.

On June 24, 1947, Kenneth Arnold, a businessman, was flying his plane near Mount Ranier, Washington. He was startled when he saw nine silver, disc-shaped objects flying through the mountains in a most spectacular manner. Arnold's sighting was reported in newspapers all over the country. The age of "flying saucers" had begun.

Arnold's report opened the way for many other reports from people who had seen what they believed were UFOs. By the end of 1947, the United States Army Air Force alone had received 122 reports. However, there were actually hundreds of other reports in the United States.

In 1967 the Center for UFO Studies published a book called *Report on the UFO Wave of 1947* by Ted Bloecher. The book listed over 850 UFO reports for 1947. The information came from newspapers and magazines throughout the United States. For the most part, these were large city newspapers and national magazines. But we know that most UFO reports are from smaller towns and rural areas. So, there had to be many more than 850 UFO reports in 1947.

On January 7, 1948, just seven months after the Ken Arnold incident, another report burst into the news.

It happened near Louisville, Kentucky. The state police received a report that a large cone-shaped, silvery object was moving slowly toward the south. The object was about 250 to 300 feet (75 to 90 meters) across.

The state police saw the object but couldn't tell what it was. So they called a nearby airport, Godman Field. The airport easily located the object. Four planes were ordered to close in on the object and find out what it was.

One plane was low on gas and had to land. The other three led by Captain Thomas Mantell, climbed high in the sky to investigate the object.

Next, two other planes had to turn back because they were running out of gas. Captain Mantell continued alone. He reported to the airport tower that the object was large and seemed to be metal. He said he was closing in on it. Suddenly he stopped transmitting. The tower could not get an answer to their calls. The next report they received was from a farmer. He said that a plane had crashed near his farmhouse. The pilot was dead.

The first Air Force reports said that what Captain Mantell had seen was the planet Venus. But while Venus can be seen in the daytime, it is only a pinpoint of light. Also, Venus does not move, and it is not cone-shaped.

After examining where the plane crashed, the Air Force did not talk about the object. It reported only that Captain Mantell had climbed to over 20,000 feet (6,100 meters). And since he had no oxygen, he passed out.

Years later it was learned that the object was a secret "sky hook" balloon being used to detect radiation.

What were all these things people were seeing? The public was crying for information. Some people in the military were also concerned. Lieutenant General Nathan F. Twining wrote a letter to the Commanding General of the Army Air Force. In the letter, he said that he thought the flying saucers seemed to be real — not fakes and not peoples' imagination. He felt that these large, disc-shaped objects could be a threat to our national defense.

As a result of all the public pressure and General Twining's letter, the Air Force felt it had to do something. On January 22, 1948, a secret operation to study UFO reports was set up. It was known as Project Sign. It was located at Wright-Patterson Air Force Base in Ohio.

Project Sign had a difficult job. During the late

These photos were taken in Canada. In the left photo, the UFO is the spot near the trees. In the right photo, it is one-third of the way down on the right side.

1940s, there were many fake UFO reports. Some people reported UFO experiences that included meeting space people and being taken aboard UFOs. In some cases, people said they were flown to Venus or some other planet. Others reported having strange physical experiences. Still others said they had been told by space people to spread the word of a new god. In these cases, there was always the hint that their leader knew some great secret that would be revealed to the world.

Certain religious groups had their own ideas about what UFOs were. Some said UFOs were God's angels giving biblical signs in the sky. Others claimed UFOs were tools of the devil trying to lead people away from God.

Occult groups reported contacts with space people through Ouija boards, séances, and spirit writing.

As time passed, the fakes were revealed for what they were. But the serious UFO reports continued to come.

During these early years of UFO history, the news media had a field day. Newspapers rushed into print with all sorts of reports. They seemed, however, to focus on the strangest cases. It was common to see such headlines as SILLY SEASON IS HERE AGAIN or UFO CHASES YOUNG GIRL. All were certain to draw the reader's attention.

Radio and TV seemed to interview the people who had had the wildest experiences. After the first sentence or two it was clear that many of these people were presented for their entertainment value, not their knowledge. They looked funny, talked funny, or dressed funny.

There were many educated people who had definite anti-UFO opinions. Most of these people had no knowledge of the facts of UFO research. But the serious research efforts went on.

On December 16, 1948, the Air Force announced the end of Project Sign. The reason given was that nothing had been found to prove or disprove the existence of UFOs. In fact, however, the project went on but with a new name: Project Grudge. Project Grudge set out to prove that there were no UFOs. In fact, the whole country seemed to be trying to explain away UFOs. The press and TV continued to present mainly the strangest, hard-to-believe reports. Also, it was often reported that UFOs were secret Air Force vehicles. In short, all of the avenues of public knowledge were used to explain away UFOs.

But UFO events continued to be reported. In 1951, Project Grudge became Project Blue Book.

By the end of 1952, the Air Force admitted to receiving 1,501 reports in that year — more than any other year. Even with all the anti-UFO publicity, reports not only continued, they increased. For the first time, the government appeared to be truly concerned.

Then another factor entered the picture. More and more reports started to come from honest, believable people. UFOs were being reported by police, astronomers and other scientists, technically trained people, air traffic controllers, airline pilots, and private pilots.

The Central Intelligence Agency (CIA) also became concerned. In 1953, the CIA formed a panel of scientists and members of various intelligence agencies. The panel was to meet for four days. The purpose was to recommend what to do about the UFO phenomenon.

The panel was chaired by Dr. H. P. Robertson, formerly of Princeton University and the California Institute of Technology. He was an expert in cosmology, mathematics, and relativity. The other members were also distinguished in their fields.

Although the meeting was supposed to be a four-day meeting, it actually sat for only 12 hours. The recommendations of this panel contained four main points.

1. Special diffraction cameras were to be used to prove to the public that the Air Force was monitoring the sky for UFOs. What looked like natural interference on radar should be treated as a UFO. Dr. J. Allen Hynek wanted an even broader program for watching the sky. But he was turned down.

2. The main source of public information on UFOs were the Aerial Phenomena Research Organization (APRO) and the Civilian Saucer Intelligence (CSI). These were private groups investigating UFO reports. It was suggested that they be watched, since they had such a strong influence on public thinking.

3. Various government agencies should take steps to convince the public that UFOs were not some sort of secret government craft.

4. The final and possibly the most important recommendation was a program to train the public to

identify objects seen in the sky. That would reduce the number of UFO reports.

Overall, however, the public increased its interest in UFOs. Radio shows, TV shows, and movies became numerous. Pressure on the government and criticism of the Air Force continued. The Air Force became worried about their image.

Dr. Hynek, drifting further from the Air Force position, wrote a letter to Colonel J. F. Spaulding. Dr. Hynek recommended that a committee of civilian scientists should review the work of Project Blue Book.

The committee was formed. The chairman was Brian O'Brian. It included five scientists: Launor Carter, Jesse Orlansky, Richard Porter, Carl Sagan, and Willis A. Ware. The meeting lasted for one day in February 1966. The committee reported that the UFO matter was being properly handled. The conclusion was that there was no threat to our national security.

The next step in UFO history came in April 1966. In that year, the first hearings on UFOs were held before the Congress. One hearing was suggested by Gerald R. Ford, Republican minority leader in the House of Representatives. Only three witnesses appeared before the committee. They were Harold D. Brown, secretary of the Air Force; Dr. J. Allen Hynek, astronomical consultant to Project Blue Book; and Major Hector Quintanilla, chief of Project Blue Book. All were associated with the Air Force. The following month the Air Force said it was seeking an independent group to conduct a scientific study of the UFO phenomenon.

For the next five months, the Air Force tried to interest several universities in taking on the job. None accepted.

Finally, on October 7, 1966, Edward U. Condon, a physicist at the University of Colorado, accepted the study project.

However, even before the study began, Dr. Condon was quoted in the press as saying that he did not believe there was life elsewhere, nor did he believe that flying saucers had visited earth.

While the staff was still at work, a second congressional hearing was held. This one at the request of J. Edward Roush, congressman from Indiana.

The hearing was before the House Science and Astronautics Committee. The hearings were broader than the previous ones. The participants included astronomers, physicists, sociologists, psychologists, engineers, and others. The discussions were often heated. Some were sure UFOs did not exist. Others were just as sure they did exist.

Meanwhile, the Condon Report was completed and given to the National Academy of Sciences for review. The review panel of 11 scientists approved the report. They said there was no reason for the government to continue the study of UFOs.

Thus, in 1969 Project Blue Book was closed. Its records were sent to Maxwell Air Force Base at Montgomery, Alabama. With proper security clearance the records were made available to the public.

The news media greatly publicized the section of the Condon Report that was Dr. Condon's personal view of the UFO phenomenon. On reading the entire report, many people were shocked to find that scientists on the committee staff did not say what Condon's summary said. It was probably this difference, that led so many scientists to take new interest in the UFO phenomenon. So, with the end of the government interest in the UFO matter, and with the growing interest of the individual scientist, this part of UFO history ends.

It is time to see what all the fuss is about. What do people report?

FOUR
What Do People Report?

In this chapter, we will describe some of the things people report most often. We will also give explanations for these things.

Most UFO sightings are reported as occurring at night. Fewer people are outdoors at night, yet most sightings occur then. Why? The main reason is that people are more aware of the night sky than the day sky. It follows that any strange event is more likely to be seen in the night sky than in the day sky.

What follows are some things people report. First, let's look at sightings that are less than 500 feet (152 meters) away.

The chart in Figure 1 shows when and how many close encounters were seen. The greatest number of sightings occur between 8:00 P.M. and midnight. Note, that not only are there the greatest number of sightings; but that all three kinds of cases, electromagnetic interference cases (CE I), physical trace cases (CE II), and the alien cases (CE III), have the

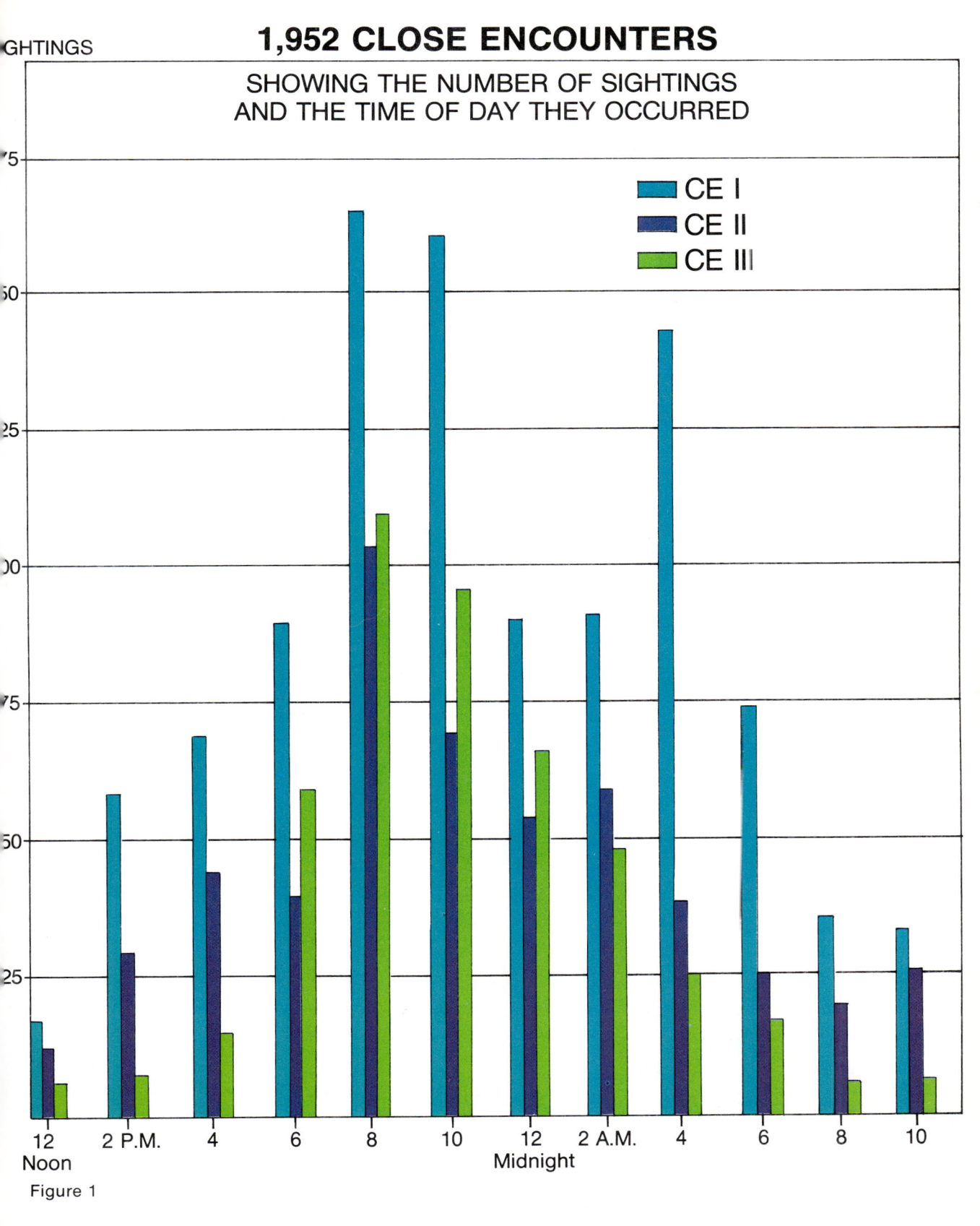
Figure 1

highest concentration in the same period.

The electromagnetic interference cases are reports that include a singularly strange effect. Automobile drivers report that in the presence of a UFO the headlights of their car dim or go out and the motor stops. Other witnesses report that the TV picture flops over.

Observers often report a very large, bright light in the night sky. They noticed it because it was bigger and brighter than the stars. And they say it didn't move like an airplane or a helicopter. Often the object seems to dart rapidly from side to side. Upon questioning the observer, it usually turns out that the large, bright light was really just a pinpoint of light. The darting back and forth of the UFO is caused by the eye. When someone stares at a small bright spot of light against a black sky, the light seems to dart back and forth.

Often a person says that the light changes color. For example, from red to green to yellow and then to blue. Actually the light source does not change color. It seems to change because near the horizon the air acts like a prism. The air bends a white light into the colors of the spectrum.

Sometimes people report a very large, bright light moving rapidly through the sky. A check usually shows that the person saw clouds moving rapidly past the moon.

Another example of bright lights is the report of a group of UFOs shooting through the northeastern sky. Research indicates that the viewers are seeing the Perseid meteor shower. It occurs each year between August 10 and 12 in the northeastern sky. It occurs after midnight about halfway above the horizon.

And so it goes with bright lights in the night sky. Almost all these night lights turn out to be normal objects or natural conditions.

Now let us move to close encounters. These are sightings that occur within about 500 feet from the person. Close encounters tell us much about the UFO phenomenon. In a Close Encounter of the First Kind (CE I), an object or a light is about 500 feet away. The observer has a good chance to see details of the UFO. Also, it is easier to tell how fast the object is moving. One can point a finger at the object and move the arm at the same rate. Later repeating the rate of motion allows an investigator to figure out the actual speed of the UFO.

Also, when an object is close, it is more likely to pass near something like a house or a tree. Again, later it will be easier to figure out the size of the UFO.

In a Close Encounter of the Second Kind (CE II), the object lands or comes near the earth. The object usually causes some sort of change in the earth's surface. There may be marks of landing legs. There could also be burned grass or bushes, or there may be a change in the soil. In a CE III, footprints of beings might remain after the UFO has left.

Figure 2 shows details of the length of the CE II reports. It also shows the percentage of the distances of the sightings. The graph shows that 40% of all reports last between one and five minutes. That is amazing when you see that the balance of the duration reports are all very close to the average.

Figure 3 is also rather startling. Forty percent of all UFOs are seen from a range of 50 feet (15 meters) or less. That is only about 20 steps away from where you are now.

The question of the color of UFOs is often raised. Figure 4 shows that most UFOs appear as metallic. Red, orange, and white follow in that order.

As you can see in Figure 5, the marks of landing legs show two, three, four, five, or six legs. Why so many?

In answer, the first thing to ask is: How many legs are required to keep the object from falling over?

The UFO report of two legs is certainly subject to question. How could a large, heavy object stand on two legs without falling down?

Three or four legs would be enough to hold up even a very heavy object. Why then do some people report five or six legs? Are these people wrong? It could be that the objects are so heavy that they need five or six legs.

It is an interesting question. And no one has the answer. All we know is what is shown in Figure 5.

The shape of the landing site is shown in Figure 6. Most (71%) UFOs on the ground are circular. The rest of the reports show oval objects (11%) and irregular objects (18%). The large number of circular objects brings us back to our last question. How could a circular object that is 30 to 50 feet (9 to 15 meters) wide balance on two legs?

Figure 7 indicates that in CE IIs, 46% of the sites had burned areas. Another 33% had a dent, and 21% showed signs of being dried out. The burned sites are most interesting. Some seem to have been burned by a flame. Yet, the fuel or the thing that was burning has never been identified.

Other reports indicate the burned areas do not seem to have been burned by a flame. Rather, the objects seem to have been subjected to great heat. The grass or plants seem to be dried up or scarred. But there has never been any evidence of large amounts of radiation.

Depressed areas are a guide to the size of the object that rested on the ground. Where dehydration is evident the ground is totally without moisture. An illustration of how a UFO landing affects the soil is shown in Figures 8 and 9.

In the left foreground of Figure 8 is black soil from Kansas. In the right foreground at the rear are clumps of brown soil only a few feet from the black soil. The brown soil was taken from the dried out, or dehy-

Figure 2

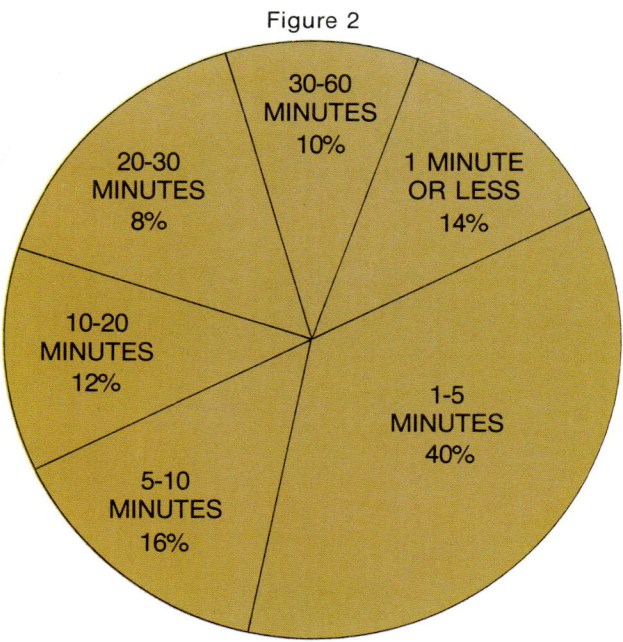

This graph shows the number of minutes people viewed UFOs in Close Encounters of the Second Kind. It also shows the percentage of each viewing time.

Figure 3

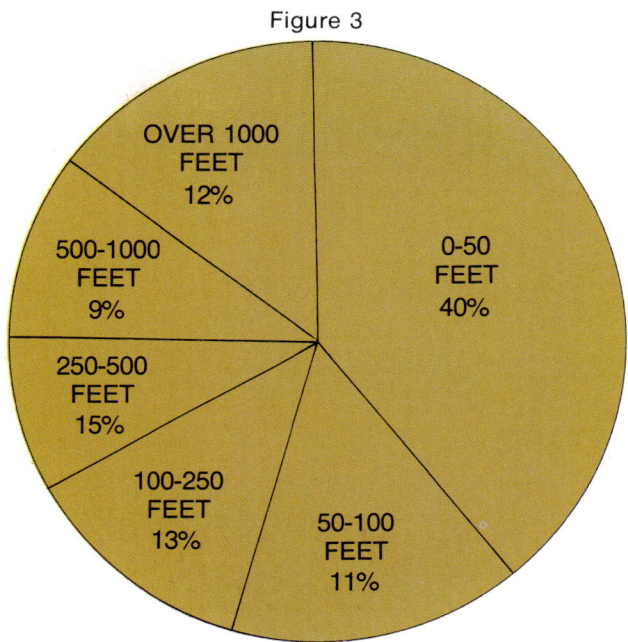

This graph shows percentages of how far people were from UFOs in CE IIs. It is surprising that most were 50 feet or closer from the UFO.

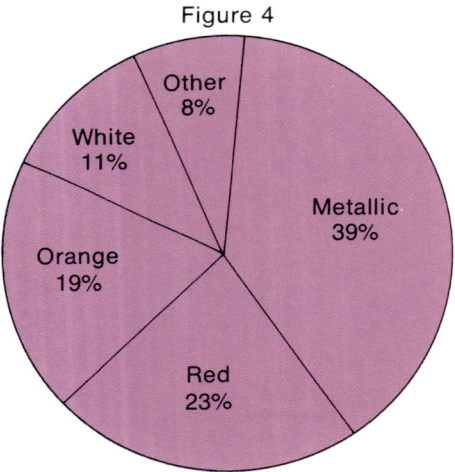

The graph above shows percentages of the four most common colors mentioned by people in UFO reports.

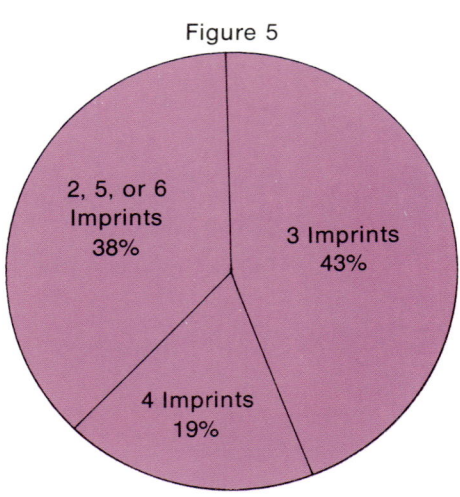

This graph shows the percentages of the number of marks made in the ground by the legs of UFOs.

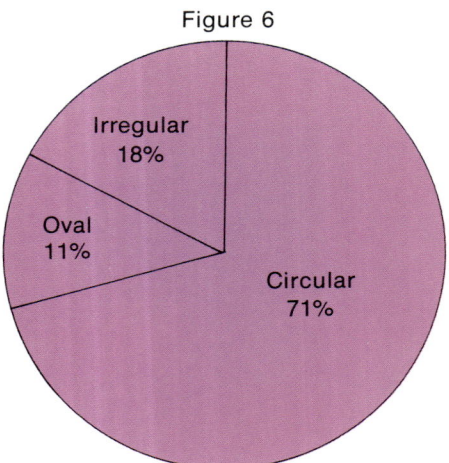

This graph shows the percentages of the shapes made in the ground by UFOs.

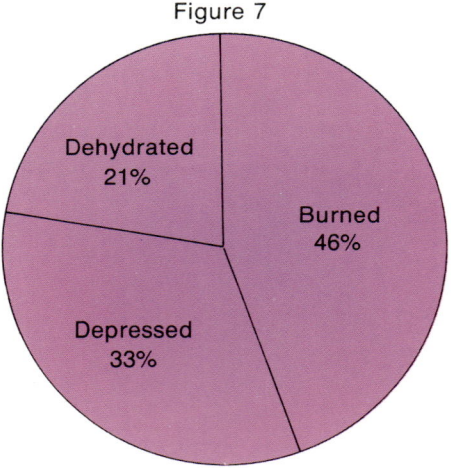

This graph shows the percentages of the effect UFOs had on the ground.

drated, ring left by a reported UFO. The soil has been changed in some way. Note that the brown soil does not absorb the drops of water.

Figure 9 illustrates the result of a laboratory experiment. Seeds were placed in the black soil (left) and the brown soil (right). Note the lack of growth of the seed in the brown soil.

We have looked at some of the things that people report. Now let's go on to what people see.

Figure 8

The brown soil, which was affected by a UFO, will not absorb water.

Figure 9

Seeds will not grow in the brown soil, which is on the right.

FIVE
What Do People See?

There is a big difference between what people report about UFOs and what people really see. Everyone who makes a report believes there was a UFO. But, as statistics show, only about 10% of all reports really turn out to be UFOs.

The following chart, taken from the "International UFO Reporter," represents a typical year of both UFOs and IFOs as reported to the Center for UFO Studies.

TOTAL NUMBER OF SIGHTINGS: 861

```
UFOs:     TOTAL—83
Nocturnal Lights ............................................... 57
Daylight Discs .................................................. 17
Radar-Visuals ...................................................  0
Close Encounter-1st Kind ......................................  5
Close Encounter-2nd Kind .....................................  1
Close Encounter-3rd Kind .....................................  3
```

IFOs: TOTAL — 778

Stars & Planets 240
Advertising Planes 179
Aircraft 106
Meteors 84
Helicopters 37
Balloons 29
Satellites 20
Moon 15
Re-entries 14
Prank Balloons 11
Searchlights 7
Flares 6
Kites 5
Missile Launches 5
Ground Lights 4
Birds 4
Airborne residue 2
Reflection 2
Lightning, Contrail, Mirage, Cloud, Tower, Visual Disorder, Moondog, Test Cloud . . . . .1 each

Let us start by examining identified flying objects (IFOs). They are the cause of most UFO reports.

I am always finding out how little the average person knows about events that occur in the sky. Two incidents come to mind.

Several years ago on a still, summer evening, I had set up my telescope on my driveway to look at the moon. A neighbor who was out to take a walk, stopped. He asked what I was looking at. I told him, "An eclipse of the moon." His reply was, "What's an eclipse?"

On another occasion, as I drove into my driveway, I glanced up over the roof of my garage to the north. There I saw the undulating waves of the northern lights (aurora borealis). This was only the second time in my life I had seen this phenomenon, so I jumped out of my car to watch the splendor. Several neighbors across the street had seen me leave my car quickly. They called over to me, "What are you looking at?"

"The aurora borealis," I called, not moving.

"You mean those lights in the sky?" they asked.

"Yes," I replied.

"That's only the neon lights from town reflecting on the clouds," they told me.

And so it goes. People don't know what they are seeing, yet they have all the answers. Thus, it is not difficult to see why most UFO reports are the result of something in the sky being mistaken for something else. In fact, most unidentified lights turn out to be the planet Venus. When Venus is rising in the early morning hours in the eastern sky under certain conditions, it appears quite large. It may even seem to be pulsating.

Figure 1 was reported to show two UFOs in the night sky over a small town in Michigan. The photographer claims the photo is not a time exposure. But the photo is clearly a time exposure of the moon and Venus and can be proved without any question.

Look at Figure 2. This time-exposure photo shows a Russian sputnik satellite as a streak through the night sky. The satellite is moving from left to right. Also shown, at the lower left, is Venus. The moon is to the right of Venus. Both are fuzzy-edged because of the time exposure. Also note that the stars in the picture are elongated. All these points indicate that the photo is a time exposure.

Suppose both Venus and the moon were in ascension. That would make an arc upward to the right that is just like the two angled lines in Figure 1. In fact, that is exactly what the two lines in Figure 1 are, Venus and the moon.

When an investigator tells a witness that the UFO he or she has reported is actually Venus, the witness

Figure 1

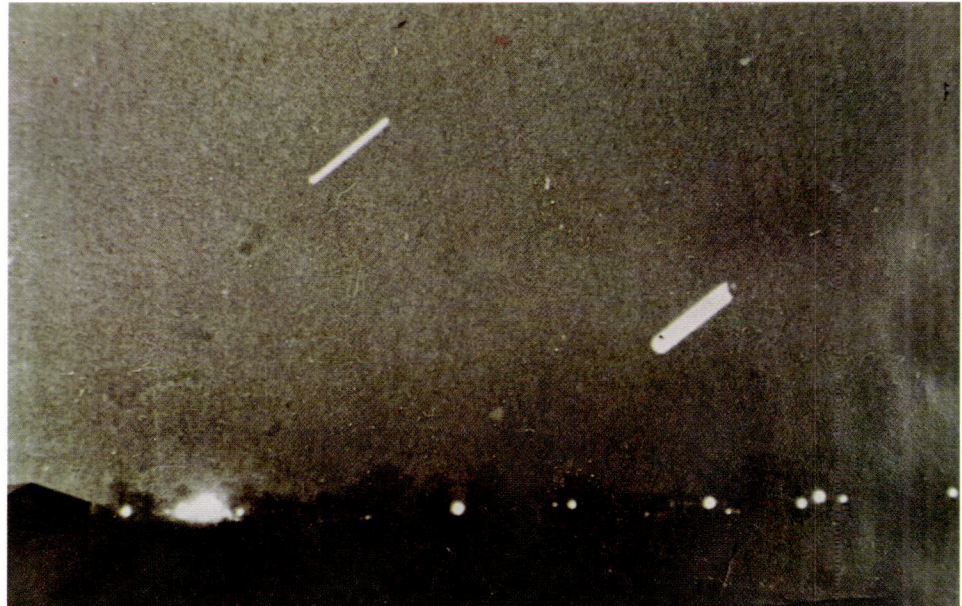

This photo was reported as a UFO. It is actually the moon and Venus.

Figure 2

This photo was also reported as a UFO. It is a Russian sputnik satellite.

often becomes angry. The explanation is not acceptable. The witness says the object was too large, too bright, and too close to be Venus. Also, it was too low in the sky to be Venus. But in most cases, it *was* Venus.

The second largest category of UFO misinterpretations are aircraft. Advertising planes, commercial, military, and private planes, and helicopters also are causes of UFO reports.

The reason people so often mistake an airplane for a UFO is because they think they always know an airplane when they see one. The truth is, many times they don't. This is proved by the great number of planes reported as UFOs. There is no other explanation.

The landing speed of most airplanes ranges from about 80 to 180 miles per hour (130 to 290 kilometers per hour). A small plane coming directly toward you would cover the last 10 miles (16 kilometers) to touchdown in just under ten minutes. A larger plane would cover the last 10 miles in just over three minutes. From a distance of 10 miles, a plane's landing lights are quite bright. A small plane coming directly toward the observer with its landing lights on, can appear to twinkle or be sending messages. For the ten minutes it takes to fly the final 10 miles, the small plane would appear to be hovering. The large plane would approach so fast that it would be easier to tell it was an airplane.

Often when a large plane flies overhead with its red Mars lights flashing and its red and green wing lights lit, a witness will often report that a triangular UFO passed. They see the lights and imagine the area between the lights as being solid.

Again, when the investigation is complete and the UFO is identified as an IFO (airplane), witnesses are unbelieving. After all, *they know what an airplane looks like!*

The next largest causes of UFO reports are meteors, weather and test balloons, satellites, the

Figure 3

Figure 4

Balloons like the two in these photographs are often mistaken for UFOs.

Figure 5

Figure 6

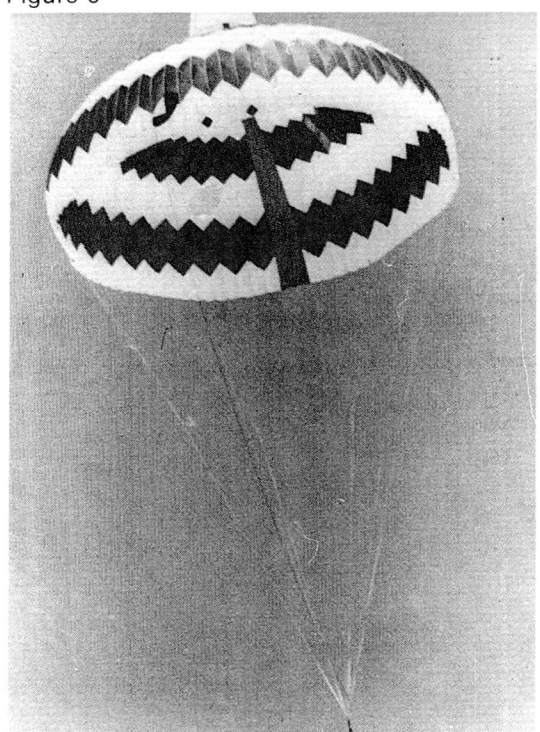

Figure 7

Figure 8

Parachutes like these four are also commonly mistaken for UFOs.

moon, satellite reentries, parachutes, and prank balloons. Figures 3 and 4 are balloons. Figures 5 through 8 are parachutes.

Searchlights used to attract attention at fairs, store openings, and the like are the cause of two different effects. The effect depends on how far the observer is from the searchlight and also on the condition of the atmosphere.

At a considerable distance on a clear but cloudy, night, the observer sees what seems to be a disc of light flying across the sky. Actually, it is the light shining on the clouds. The beam is not visible because of the clear air. When the air is not clear and the observer is near the searchlight, the reports describe a UFO (the light on the clouds) with a beam of light shining earthward. The beam is caused by the light being reflected off particles in the unclear air.

Flares that are either dropped from small planes or attached to balloons are also reported as UFOs. The flare dropped from a plane will drift with the wind as it comes to earth. The balloon, on the other hand, rises as the heat of the flare warms the air in the balloon. Often as the balloon rises, it moves through the layers of winds blowing in different directions. That causes the balloon to change direction.

Kites and birds also seem to dart about, because they are also strongly affected by winds. Kites may be in the form of birds, planes, dragons, rockets, or even discs. They are the objects of fewer UFO reports, yet they are reported.

The large number of UFO reports that turn out to be IFOs does not bother the investigator. Remember that if it were not for the public response, there would be *no* reports.

The fact that most UFO reports are in fact IFOs, does not in any way take away from the real UFO reports.

SIX

How Do Researchers Study a UFO Report?

To the strong believer in UFOs, Project Blue Book said too many UFOs were IFOs. And when a private UFO group found that a UFO was an IFO, that group was accused of going along with the Air Force. The believers felt that both groups were whitewashing UFOs.

To those who did not believe in UFOs, the opposite was true. These disbelievers did not *want* to accept the research of Project Blue Book or any other group. Sometimes the disbelievers ignored facts of UFO reports or even gave their own interpretations of the reports. They tried to explain away all UFOs.

All of this confusion, on both sides, is mainly due to the unawareness of the general public and, in some cases professional scientists, of the costly, time-consuming, and frustrating research work done on each report.

As an example of this condition, let me relate an experience we continually encounter with the news media.

A UFO flap occurs. Within a few hours, the various news media call. They want to know things like,

"What was it?" "Where was it from?" "Why is it here?" The news media want quick answers for a quick story.

Actually, the investigation of a UFO report may take months of hard work. Only then can these answers be given. With this in mind, let's look at the work of a UFO researcher.

As we said before, with one possible exception, there are no actual UFOs to study. What is studied are the narrative reports of witnesses. What we will talk about here is a nocturnal light (NL).

The UFO report usually describes the object's shape, color, size, movements, and location in the sky. Some of these characteristics, or perhaps several of them, may alert the researcher to possible explanation of the sighting.

Most NLs are reported as lights low in the night sky. In such a case, the researcher's first job would be to find out whether the light could have been a star or a planet.

Using the time and the location of the NL, the researcher turns to his sky chart. He or she would check to see if any star or planet was supposed to be where the NL was seen. Most NLs are identified as IFOs in this way.

Often, when a witness is told that the NL is a star or planet, he or she will not accept it. It is amazing how unaware people are of the tricks the atmosphere and the eye can play. Many people do not know how a planet moves across the sky from east to west. A planet appears low in the eastern sky. It rises and then goes down in the western sky. Planets that are near the horizon look brighter and larger because of the dense atmosphere. Some observers report that the light changes color. The light is not really changing color. It only seems to change color. The effect is caused by the reaction of the light as it passes through the earth's

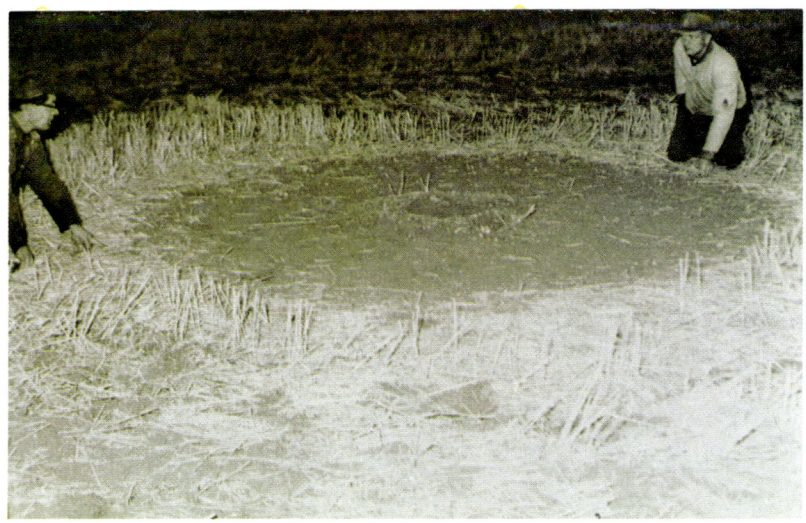

The above photo shows the oval-shaped mark made in the ground by a UFO.

atmosphere. We call that twinkling. Another thing that makes the light seem to change is rising columns of warm air. Warm air can cause some stars to twinkle, while others do not.

The darting motion often described in NL reports is a trick of the eye. When a single bright light is viewed against a black background, the light appears to wander or dart about.

If the sky charts do not show a star or planet where the NL was seen, it is necessary to investigate another possibility. The researcher next may check planes and helicopters. Airplane and helicopter lights are the second most common source of UFO reports.

People usually think of airplanes as things that move rapidly through the sky. When a light moves through the sky in a way different from a person's idea of how a plane looks, he or she might think it was a UFO.

Airplane landing lights are extremely bright. The landing lights of a large plane are more than four times brighter than an automobile headlight. If one airplane with only one landing light was 100 miles (161 kilome-

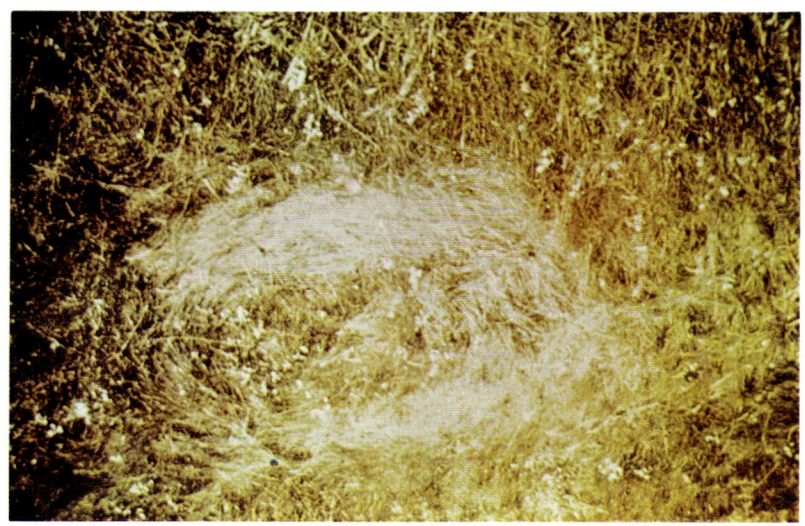
This photograph shows the effect a UFO had on the ground.

ters) away, the light would be the brightest one in the sky. If an airplane were coming toward a person, the light would seem to stand still for the time it would take the plane to fly the 100 miles. If the light suddenly went out, it could be because the plane turned. And if all this were seen before the plane was close enough to hear its engines, witnesses might easily make a UFO report.

To check this report, the researcher would contact a Federal Aviation Agency (FAA) control center. The local airport control tower might also be checked. Both the usual and unusual traffic would be checked. However, if the FAA cannot confirm an NL as a plane, the researcher might still classify the report as an IFO because it fits all of the descriptions of a plane.

Helicopters can hover and move horizontally and vertically. There are often reports of a very bright light beaming down to the earth. Many helicopters have a powerful light mounted beneath them. Police use the light to seek out criminal suspects. Military helicopters use the light for rescue work, and so on.

Many witnesses have reported a slow-moving NL

This photograph was taken in Delphos, Kansas. It shows the mark of a UFO.

followed by a band of flashing lights. To the researcher, a common explanation is an advertising plane. These are small, low-flying planes. Under the wings they have hundreds of small lights. These lights spell out the advertising message of a company. From directly below the plane, a person could read the words. However, from an angle the words could not be read. The plane would look like a lot of moving, flashing lights. There are dozens of companies that have such planes. A phone call to the nearest aerial display company can determine the location, time, and date of their planes. These planes cause a great number of UFOs to become IFOs.

We have discussed some of the common explanations of NLs. When the NL does not fit any of these, the researcher must look for other causes. Relying on the witness's report and experience in investigating thousands of reports, the researcher turns his attention to balloons, satellites, clouds, or several other possibilities.

If the light or object resembles the slow, steady motion of a floating balloon, the researcher can call the local airport. The airport will know about balloon launches. The National Weather Service may also be checked to see if the reported object is a weather balloon. Weather balloons are launched twice a day from certain places.

Flashes of light that last two seconds or less are probably meteors. They can easily be checked on meteor charts. Long flashes of light, perhaps a minute or longer, are probably from a satellite, or a part of one, burning as it enters the earth's atmosphere. A call to North American Air Defense (NORAD), which tracks all satellites, satellite parts, and space debris, will solve that problem. Satellites look like bright lights moving rapidly in straight lines at very high altitudes. The Smithsonian Institution has a record of the satellite schedule.

Clouds are sometimes mistaken for UFOs. Usually, two kinds of clouds are involved. The first kind is called a lenticular cloud. It is shaped like a lens. At times, these lens-shaped clouds can look like disc-shaped objects rather than clouds.

The second kind of cloud that is mistaken for a UFO is a test cloud. Test clouds are formed by exploding a special capsule in the upper atmosphere. These clouds are used in scientific testing. Their locations can be checked through various government agencies.

Other possible causes of UFO reports that a researcher considers include reflections, searchlights, flares, mirages, ground lights, lightning, birds, and kites.

What you have read in this chapter is only a small sample of what a researcher does. Finding out whether some object is really a UFO may take hours, days, or even months of very hard work. But the reason for all this work is to be absolutely sure that what is called a UFO *is* a UFO. The reports in the next chapter are such cases.

SEVEN

Some UFO Cases

The UFO cases in this chapter are presented for the purpose of education. These cases will help you understand the kinds of details that are in high-quality UFO cases. All these reports went through the research process outlined in Chapter 6. Using those standards, the reports became UFO cases.

The details of these cases are from the files of the Center for UFO Studies. The cases were published in the *International UFO Reporter,* a news publication to which the Center contributes information. These are all close encounter cases.

As you might expect, most of the cases are CE Is. CE IIs come next. CE IIIs are last.

CLOSE ENCOUNTER OF THE FIRST KIND (CE I)

A CE I is the experience of seeing an object in the sky, during daylight hours or at night, in which the object is 500 feet (152 meters) or less from the observer.

PLACE
Connecticut

CONDITIONS
Midsummer. Weekday afternoon. Calm, clear sky.

WITNESSES
Thirteen boys, 14 and 15 years old. Camp counselor, age 23.

DESCRIPTION OF OBJECT
Flat-bottomed saucer with a red half-dome on top. Metallic silver color, shiny smooth texture. No features seen. A purple haze surrounded the object. No heat or odor was reported. The object was about 20 feet (6 meters) in diameter.

SIGHTING DETAILS
The witnesses heard a high-pitched whine. When they looked up through a clearing in the trees, they saw the object. It hovered for 15 to 25 seconds. Then there was another high whine, and the object rose and disappeared.

PLACE
Idaho

CONDITIONS
Winter. Weekday night. Clear, calm, cold.

WITNESSES
One witness 60 feet (18.3 meters) away. Second witness several miles away.

DESCRIPTION OF OBJECT

The object was oval, without any detail. The observer who was 60 feet away said the object was light green. There were occasional flashes of white, orange, and pink lights. The object made no noise when it was still but whistled when it moved.

SIGHTING DETAILS

The object rose from behind some trees. It hovered at treetop height for three minutes. When it left, it took about 15 seconds to move out of sight. A witness 10 miles (16 kilometers) away, reported the same object. He said that it hovered for about 10 minutes and then left, going upward.

PLACE
Pennsylvania

CONDITIONS

Spring. Weekday evening. Clear sky. Winds from the west at seven miles per hour (11 kilometers per hour).

WITNESSES

Eleven witnesses in six different groups.

DESCRIPTION OF OBJECT

A red ball of fire the size of the moon. The object made no noise. There was no evidence of heat or odor.

SIGHTING DETAILS

The object was a few hundred feet in the air. It moved from north to south above the witnesses' homes. The sighting lasted two to five minutes. It silently swayed like a falling leaf. It dropped down to land near a house. It burned the grass over an area of 100 feet by 30 feet (30.5 by 9 meters). The object made two holes. One was 1 inch (2.5 centimeters) deep and 2½ inches (6.4 centimeters) across. The other hole was 3 inches (7.6 centimeters) deep and 12 inches (30.5 centimeters) across.

PLACE
    California

CONDITIONS
    Fall. Night. Clear sky.

WITNESSES
    One witness about 55 feet (16.8 meters) away. Six other witnesses at about one mile (1.6 kilometers) away.

DESCRIPTION OF OBJECTS
    One object was overhead. Two others were seen at a distance. The near object was shaped like a shallow bowl with a dome. The dome had ribs running up and down. Both the dome and base were a dark silver-gray. The upper part looked liked porcelain. The outer rim looked like stainless steel. The rim rotated clockwise. The underside was flat and had a white light in the center. When the object hovered, the light was dim. When the object moved, the light became bright. The outer part of the flat underside turned slowly counterclockwise. There were six cables hanging from the object. They were about 7 feet (2 meters) long and 2½ inches (6.4 centimeters) thick. The ends of the cables were frayed. At the edge of the underside, there were hooklike arms.

SIGHTING DETAILS

The first witness had a power failure in his mobile home. When he stepped outside to check on it, he noticed that his body was electrically charged because his hair was standing on end. He looked up and saw the object. It was about 55 feet (16.8 meters) above him. He was able to tell the distance because of the farm buildings and TV antenna nearby. The object hovered, then slowly moved westward. As the object moved over a barn, the cables retracted to avoid touching the roof. The object moved about the neighborhood for some 20 minutes. The witness and his wife and two children then drove to a friend's house about two miles (3.2 kilometers) away. His friends, a man and woman, also had seen the object. Three other witnesses also reported seeing objects in the sky.

CLOSE ENCOUNTER OF THE SECOND KIND (CE II)

A CE II is like a CE I, but the object comes near the earth or lands. There is an interaction with the surface. This might include foliage being burned or shriveled and a chemical or structural change in the soil.

PLACE
Iowa

CONDITIONS
Fall. Early evening. Clear night.

WITNESS
One woman.

DESCRIPTION OF OBJECT
A dark, horizontal oval with two brilliant white lights flashing on and off. It came directly toward the witness. There was no sound.

SIGHTING DETAILS

The object rose from behind distant trees and came toward the witness. As it came near, her FM radio went silent. The woman was a guard at a factory. She tried to call other guards, but her walkie-talkie did not work. The object passed near a streetlamp, and when the object's lights shined on it, the streetlamp went out. When the UFO passed, it seemed to drop down into a farm area across the street. After the object was out of sight, the woman's walkie-talkie worked and she called other guards. The farmer on whose land the object seemed to have landed was not aware of the object. But he said that his TV blacked out for a minute or two.

PLACE
New Mexico

CONDITIONS
Fall. Midafternoon. Very thin cloud cover.

WITNESS
One person.

DESCRIPTION OF OBJECT
Flat, silver gray, domed disc. It seemed to be five to six times wider than the sun.

SIGHTING DETAILS
The object moved in level flight. Then suddenly turned upward and disappeared. The object was estimated at one half mile (.8 kilometer) away.

**CLOSE ENCOUNTER
OF THE THIRD KIND (CE III)**

A CE III has CE I and CE II characteristics, but the

witness has an encounter with an alien, either outside or inside the object.

PLACE
   Kentucky

CONDITIONS
   Winter. Night.

WITNESSES
   Three women.

DESCRIPTION OF OBJECT
   A saucer with a glowing white dome. A row of red lights around the middle and three or four red and yellow lights underneath. The size was reported from "equal to two houses" to "as big as a football field."

SIGHTING AND CONTACT DETAILS
   The object flew down to treetop level about 100 yards (90 meters) away from the witnesses. It circled behind them and apparently took control of their car. Later all the witnesses were hypnotized. Their reports were very similar. The aliens were four feet (122 centimeters) tall, and they were dark. The witnesses were taken aboard the craft. The aliens gave them a thorough examination and then released them. The witnesses were later examined. They had burn marks on the backs of their necks, and their exposed skin was blistered. Their eyes burned and teared. They had lost a lot of weight.

PLACE
   Kansas

CONDITIONS
Midsummer. Weekday night. Clear, high fluffy clouds.

WITNESSES
Two married adults ages 18 and 19, and their infant child.

DESCRIPTION OF OBJECT
Witnesses saw a group of three UFOs followed by a group of four. All were followed by one other low-flying UFO. Later, under hypnosis, the low-flying UFO was described as two huge pie plates joined at the rim. The object was about 40 feet (12 meters) high and 150 feet (46 meters) wide. Two rings, one above and one below the rim, rotated clockwise.

SIGHTING AND CONTACT DETAILS
While driving home in the country, the witnesses noticed a light low in the sky near the road. For some reason, they pulled the car off the road. They saw the object ahead. They left their car and their baby and walked up to the object. It was about two to four stories high. They walked up a shiny metal step and entered the object. The inside looked like a control area. It had computerlike equipment and flashing lights. The two were put into separate rooms. There they saw aliens 5 feet 6 inches (168 centimeters) tall. The aliens performed several physical tests, using needles, tubes, and other things. They were later helped out of the craft, and they returned to their car. They later noticed there were many marks and bruises on their bodies.

The following three reports are from foreign countries. They were chosen to show how widespread the UFO phenomenon is. The first is a CE I. The other two are CE IIIs.

PLACE
Brazil

WITNESSES
Three men. A woman. Several squads of police.

SIGHTING DETAILS
Three men watched a dense, white cloud hover low over the street. The cloud faded and a flying disc was revealed. The men watched as light beams of various colors were emitted. A woman watching from a window called police. Several squads arrived. With pistols drawn one shouted, "We're the police!" All were suddenly paralyzed. The cloud reappeared, enveloped the disc, and all disappeared.

PLACE
Iran

WITNESSES
A man and woman.

SIGHTING AND CONTACT DETAILS
A glittering object landed 100 feet (30.5 meters) in front of the witnesses' car. It was disc-shaped and about 47½ feet (14.5 meters) across. There was a small window in the side. Inside were two aliens that looked like Egyptian mummies.

PLACE
France

DESCRIPTION OF OBJECT
An orange, dome-shaped glimmer on a road.

This is one of several photographs taken in Brazil of a UFO.

WITNESS
One woman. (She could recall the event only under hypnosis.)

SIGHTING DETAILS
A young woman was driving from the town to her farm. Her car misfired, stalled, and the lights went out. Under hypnosis she revealed that she saw two dwarfs that had large eyes and were dressed in black overalls. They carried her to the light and entered through a door. She was placed on a table, and handcuffs were put on her ankles and wrists. After an examination, she was released and the craft rose and disappeared. She entered her car, and it started at once. She continued to her home. She found that her trip had taken two hours longer than it normally would have.

In Chapter 2, we said that no government or group had in its possession a UFO or a part of a UFO. The following UFO report may now change that.

The story begins in 1950. A book published in that year told of a UFO that had crashed in the Southwest. The story had no details and no names of witnesses. The report was later proved to be a fake. But over the years, the story came up again and again.

Then in 1978 the Center for UFO Studies investigated a UFO crash that took place at about the same time and in the same general area as the 1950 fake. But there was a difference. This time there were witnesses' names, the date, and other information. And the details of the crash were very different from those of the fake.

Here is the story. UFO investigators recently met a man who had been checking into the old report of the UFO in the Southwest. The man had first heard the story about 25 years ago. He was serving in Korea with the National Security Agency. A friend of his, a sergeant, told him the incident. The sergeant's uncle, who was then a major, was a member of a UFO chase group. On one occasion he was chasing a UFO in the Southwest. The UFO crashed and was half buried in the sand. The major landed the plane as close to the crash as possible. But when he and his radar operator got there, they saw a lot of police and soldiers. The two were not allowed to go near the object. And they saw that a cover had been put over it. Soon more soldiers arrived. They lifted the object onto a truck and drove away.

The man has since found his sergeant friend again. He has also talked to the sergeant's uncle. And he knows the name of the military base from which the trucks came to get the UFO. An officer from the base would not discuss the incident, but he did not deny it.

The Center for UFO Studies has tape recordings of witnesses. They have confirmed many details of the incident. The Center is now producing — with another organization — two long-playing records that include this incident. Some of the information has not been completely checked. For example, the Center is looking for a scientist who was said to have examined the UFO. When all the sources have been checked and all the details confirmed, we may have our first UFO.

EIGHT
If You See a UFO

The suggestions in this chapter will help you get the most accurate details if you have a UFO experience. These are the kinds of things the scientific researcher needs to make a good evaluation of your report.

In one sense, this chapter is just short of ridiculous. Why? Because you don't know how you would react if you had a close encounter. Also, you wouldn't be able to remember most of the suggestions.

So, just read the suggestions and the reasons for them so that you have a better understanding of why you should do these things. Most of the suggestions are put as questions. Pretend you are asking yourself these questions.

With this background, let us set up the situation for your sighting.

You and two friends are outdoors. It is daytime, and you are standing in your backyard talking. You glance off into the distance and see something. Because you are talking, you don't pay close attention to what you see. You look up again. This time the object is over some nearby trees. You stop and point at the object and say, "Hey, what in the world is that?" The other two look and also see the object. It is moving toward the group. Now it is within 500 feet (152 meters). You are having a CE I.

Close Encounter of the First Kind

How close is 500 feet? If you live in the city, that would be about 16 houses away. If you live in the suburbs, it would be about 6 houses away.

At this point you would start to react. How is your mind and body reacting to what your eyes are seeing? Are you awed? Frightened? Worried?

Now, you should start to think about details of the object. First think about how the object looks — its shape, color, and size. Consider how it is moving. Does it seem to be controlled? Or is it drifting? Watch how it flies. Is it wobbling, zigzagging, moving from side to side, darting, rising and falling? Or is it flying straight? If it is near something, remember that thing. Then, later you will be able to tell exactly how far away the object was.

Think about how high in the air the object is. Again, not in feet, but in relation to something. For example, the height of a tree, roof of a house, or a telephone pole. Another way to judge the height is to point at the object. Remember the position of your arm. Later you can imitate the position, and that will help an investigator figure out the height.

You should try to time how long you see the object. That is, from when you first see it until it disappears from view. If you have a watch, check the time. Otherwise you can count with an even tempo. This tempo can be repeated later for investigators. When you lose sight of the object, check your watch again or remember your last number.

This photograph shows the mark made by a landing leg of a UFO. The UFO landed in Socorro, New Mexico.

In addition to noting how the object was moving, think about what the object did. For example, did it pass directly in front of anything? Did it seem to be going to a particular place? Did it stop at a particular point? When it came near something, did it move over the thing or around it?

Now the object comes near the ground or lands. You are now having a CE II.

Close Encounter of the Second Kind

First, let's say the object does not actually land. Remember how close to the ground it came. If it touched the ground, remember whether it touched the ground once, twice, or more times. Especially note whether the object did anything to the ground. Were the grass, leaves, or soil disturbed? If it touched, was it a gentle touch or a hard one? Did the object appear to be heavy and cumbersome or light and graceful? Did it make any sound while it was coming down?

Now the object lands. Stop counting but remember the number. Now start counting again at 1, so you can record how long it was on the ground. When it lifts off, stop that count and pick up where you left off when the object landed.

Think about how the object landed. Did it settle gently? Or did it bump down? If it had legs, count them and remember whether they all touched the ground at the same time. Note how far the object was from you.

Now that the object is down, again note whether there was any sound or movement. If there was any light coming from the object, note the color or colors. Next think about what the object was made of. Was the shell thick or thin? Did it seem to be metal, plastic, or something else? Could you see any detail of the body surface? Was it smooth, rough, seamed, or riveted? Were there any slots, indentations, protrusions, or openings of any kind?

Now you should try to figure the width and height of the object. Think in terms of, say, "From that tree to that tree," and "From the ground up to that branch." Or use any other nearby objects. These can all be measured later.

If you should be present at a CE III, there are other kinds of questions to be answered.

Close Encounter of the Third Kind

How did the alien or aliens become visible to you? If there was a door, note where the door was and whether there was any sound as it opened. If the aliens came out, it is helpful to know whether the opening stayed open or if it closed behind them. How many aliens were there?

It is very important to remember what the aliens looked like. Note their height, and get a description of their head, face, ears, neck, body, hands, legs, and feet. Also, pay close attention to their clothing. Remember whether they wore hats, belts, gloves, and shoes.

How did they move? Did they walk like humans? Did they separate or stay in a group? Did they communicate with each other in any way? Was there any sound when they moved?

Try to figure out what the aliens were doing outside the object. And watch how they return to the object. Did it seem as though they were ordered back? Did they see you? If they did, notice whether they seemed to be running away from you. If they took anything from earth back with them, remember what they took.

And now the UFO rises from the earth to leave.

As the object rose, was there any sound? Was the takeoff level or did the object swing or sway? Did the object just move away until it was too distant to be seen? Or did it dissolve before your eyes?

Now, let's talk a bit about photographs of UFOs. When I lecture, I am always asked why there are so few pictures of UFOs and why there are no really good pictures. My answer includes several points.

When people have a close encounter with a UFO, they are usually so emotionally involved that even if they have a camera, they forget to use it. When they do think of the camera, they become so excited they cannot hold the camera steady. The pictures are then fuzzy. Also, often the photographer tries to move the camera to follow the object. This, too, results in blurred pictures.

Finally, remember that most UFO sightings are at night or at a time when the light is poor.

There is no way that you or anyone else could remember to do all the things in this chapter. But these are the things you *should* look for. If you use these suggestions as a guide, the information you give to the investigator will be the right information.

This photograph was taken in Horn, Iowa.
It shows the mark left in a soybean field by a UFO.

NINE
Conclusion

Now it is time to look over all we have discussed. We will look at what we know about UFOs and the people who claim to have had a personal experience with a UFO. We will also look at the evidence we have and what can be done with it. Then we will turn to the question of what we can do about the UFO mystery. And we will also look at what scientists can do to help. We should not forget the government and what it can do to help answer the question "What is a UFO?"

It is proper to say that we know a great deal about UFOs. First, we know that UFOs are reported by people of practically every country of the world. These reports have been made for a number of years.

So our first UFO evidence is the tens of thousands of reports that have been made in the past years. These reports contain an even larger amount of information on the experiences of individuals and their UFO encounters. These reports are not simply thousands of bits of different information. They form a pattern. The fact that there is a pattern is our second piece of evidence. The patterns can tell us what to look for. They also can tell us where to look, and sometimes even when to look for UFO encounters. Another piece of evidence that there are UFOs is the fact that in spite of all efforts to show that there are no UFOs, reports keep being made. There is also some important physical evidence of UFOs. We know that there have been marks on people's bodies. Also, there has been plant damage and soil changes. There has also been some evidence of animal reactions and electrical interference. Finally, there are the photos of UFOs. There have been many fake UFO pictures. There have also been many UFO pictures that were later identified as natural objects. But there are still those photos that cannot be explained.

So, we know a lot. But what should we do about it? What can we do not only to keep the subject alive but to move to some conclusion? There are many possibilities. A first step could be to look at the UFO scientific study groups. Perhaps the best way to decide which group is doing the best work is to ask how good their scientific studies are. All these groups need help. They need help from workers, and they need money to do their job. You could offer to work part-time for a UFO group. There are always letters to be written, filing, recording, answering the phone, and many other tasks to be done. And someone has to do them. Maybe you can just stay home and clip newspaper and magazine articles. Or you could go to a library to help research information. You could even be a field investigator if you have the right training. So why not help? People can give money to their favorite group. Even buying a subscription to a publication helps.

The scientific community really became aware of the importance of UFOs when the "Scientific Report

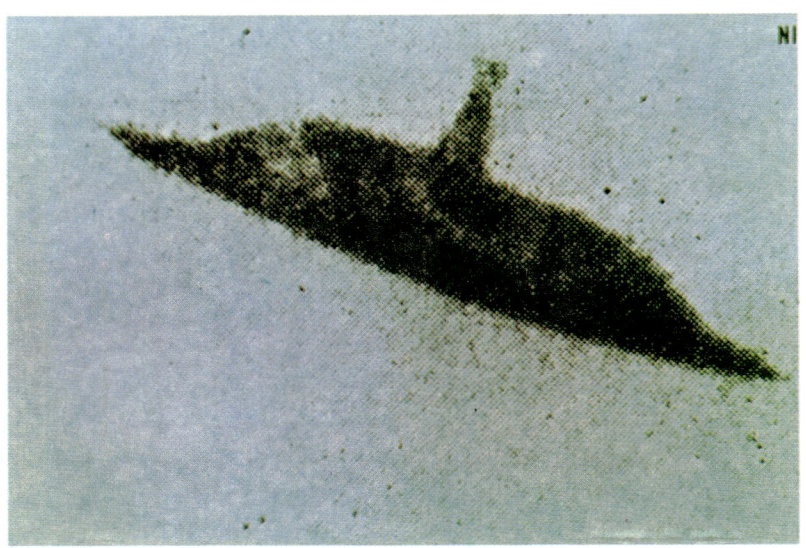

This photo is an enlargement of the UFO in the top of the picture on page 72. The photo was taken by a farmer in Oregon.

on Unidentified Flying Objects" was published. It was the report of a number of scientists who made independent studies for Dr. Edward U. Condon. When scientists read it they quickly found that the scientific papers in the report did not agree with the negative conclusions of Dr. Condon. The result was that individual scientists expressed an interest. Soon serious scientific reports were being made. Scientists have a different problem from the average person in the UFO field. They, too, could do the kinds of things individuals can. But that would be a waste of their expertise. Also, there is little money available for UFO research. Even so, scientists are submitting proposals on ways to continue UFO research. If money were available, productive research could be accomplished. At this time, aside from personal interest and study of available material, about all a scientist can do is to speak out on what could be done in the field of UFO research.

The United States government began investigations in 1947. The work continued until 1969. The

This photo was taken in France by a French Air Force officer. Note the similarity between it and the one on page 70.

conclusion was that "there was no evidence of a threat to our national security." Even though UFOs may not be a threat, UFOs should be the concern of some agency in the government. Actually, UFOs should be the concern of all governments. If the government did not want to do actual UFO research, it could sponsor a private UFO group.

Now let us consider what we, the interested public, have learned about UFOs and why the government should be interested.

    1. UFOs are reported to be able to maneuver far in excess of any earth craft.

    2. UFOs can attain speeds that allow them to appear and disappear almost instantly.

    3. UFOs have "invaded" our air space, and they have landed on the earth. In some cases, they have caused fear in our people and animals. UFOs have damaged plant life and changed the soil. Some of this

The UFO near the top of this photograph is the same one that appears on page 70.

soil beneath a UFO did not nourish plant life for long periods of time after the incident. Sometimes the change was so great that laboratory studies show that the structure of the soil is so changed that its new construction is not listed in any scientific catalog.

These three items alone should be of concern to any government.

It would be very helpful to establish a UFO communications network. This network could then track and study each UFO that is seen. If there is a UFO landing, the area should come under intensive study by the best laboratory equipment and people in the world.

The government would not have to train people for this purpose. There are already scientists personally active in the UFO field. Qualified investigators are virtually everywhere in the United States. And excellent researchers are presently active and available.

UFOCAT, the data bank created by Dr. David

Saunders, is now the property of the Center for UFO Studies. It contains about 100,000 entries. It is without question the most complete UFO record available. But even this data bank does not contain all reports known to exist. Other UFO organizations the world over have their own files.

The question arises, If we have so many cases and so much data, why don't we know what a UFO is? Why go on?

But there is a purpose. We might also say we have been working on a cure for cancer for years, and we still have no solution. Should we quit? Sometimes, in just one UFO report, there will be that one piece of information that directs us to a solution of some problem. Another question is, do all of these tens of thousands of reports prove that UFOs exist? The answer is no. But, the continuing flow of reports does establish new facts and confirm previous bits of information.

We have all this information, but we are puzzled and frustrated because we still don't understand the thing we are studying.

We have no solution to the UFO phenomenon. We must stop laughing and start listening. We must stop arguing. We must be patient. We must not give up. Each new fact adds a piece to the UFO puzzle.

Pronunciation Key

a	cat, bad
ā	able, train, play
ä	father, car
e	bet, bent
ē	me, feel, beat, piece, heavy
i	in, pig
ī	ice, time, tie, my
ō	old, goat, slow, toe
ô	paw, all, cloth, caught
oo	good, put
o͞o	tool, blue
oi	oil, toy
ou	out, plow
yo͞o	use, few
ə	up, gun, other, again, broken, pencil, button, lettuce
ər	paper, further
ch	such
ng	sing
sh	shell, wish
th	three, bath
<u>th</u>	that, together
zh	vision

Glossary

Aerial Phenomena Research Organization (APRO). a private UFO organization that investigates UFO reports.

alien (ā′ lē ən). a being seen in a Close Encounter of the Third Kind.

astronomer (ə strän′ ə mər). a person who studies the universe.

atmosphere (at′ mə sfir′). the air surrounding the earth.

aurora borealis (ə rōr′ ə bōr′ ē al′ əs). a band of bright light seen in the northern sky at night. The aurora borealis is also called the northern lights.

blip (blip). an image, or picture, on a radar screen.

cave drawing (kāv′ drô ing). drawings found on the walls of caves used by people hundreds of thousands of years ago.

CE I. *See* Close Encounter of the First Kind.

CE II. *See* Close Encounter of the Second Kind.

CE III. *See* Close Encounter of the Third Kind.

Center for UFO Studies. an organization that studies UFO reports. The Center is also a public source for UFO information.

Central Intelligence Agency (CIA). an agency of the U.S. government that makes and studies intelligence reports on foreign countries.

characteristic (kar′ ik tə ris′ tik). a special feature of something.

Civilian Saucer Intelligence (CIS). a private UFO organization that investigates UFO reports.

clockwise (kläk′ wīz). moving in the same direction as the hands of a clock.

close encounter (klōs′ in koun′ tər). a sighting of a UFO in which the UFO is 500 feet (152 meters) or less from the observer.

Close Encounter of the First Kind (CE I). the sighting of a UFO in which the observer sees details of the UFO.

Close Encounter of the Second Kind (CE II). the sighting of a UFO that lands or comes near the ground. Usually, the UFO is reported to have affected the earth in some way in a CE II.

Close Encounter of the Third Kind (CE III). a UFO sighting like a CE I and CE II, but the observer also sees aliens in the UFO.

computer (kəm pyoot′ ər). an electronic device that can store, bring back, and process information.

conclusion (kən kloo′ zhən). the end of something.

cosmology (käz mäl′ ə jē). the study of the beginnings and the structure of the universe.

counterclockwise (kount′ ər kläk′ wīz′). moving in the opposite direction of the hands of a clock.

data bank (dāt′ ə bangk). a collection of information.

daylight disc (DD) (dā′ līt disk). an object seen during the day. The observer cannot tell how far away the DD is.

DD. *See* daylight disc.

dehydration (dē′ hī drā′ shən). the taking away of all water from something.

diameter (dī am′ ət ər). the length of a straight line drawn through the center of something in the shape of a circle.

disc (disk). a thin, round-shaped object.

duration (doo rā′ shən). the time during which something lasts.

eclipse (i klips′). an eclipse occurs when one body completely or partly blocks the view of another body. For example, when the moon is directly between the earth and the sun, the moon blocks our view of the sun.

electromagnetic interference (i lek′ trō mag net′ ik int ər fir′ əns). something that causes things like radio or television sets not to work properly.

elongated (i lông′ gāt əd). stretched out.

engineer (en jən ir′). a person who uses science and mathematics to make products useful to people.

evaluation (i val′ yə wā′ shən). the study of something to find out the value or worth of the thing.

evidence (ev′ əd əns). something that can give proof of something else.

expertise (ek spər tēz′). skill or know-how in some field.

Federal Aviation Agency (FAA). the U.S. government agency that regulates airplanes and flying.

flap (flap). a large number of UFO sightings. Flaps usually occur in a rather short time in a small geographical area.

flying saucer (flī′ ing sô′ sər). a popular name given to UFOs.

foliage (fō′ lē ij). a group of leaves, flowers, and branches.

Gallup poll. a poll taken by the Gallup organization. Questions are asked of a number of people in order to find out what the public's opinion of something is.

ground lights (ground līts). the lights on the runway of an airport. Some ground lights flash, others stay on all the time.

horizon (hə rīz′ ən). the place where the earth seems to meet the sky.

horizontal (hōr ə zänt′ əl). running in the same direction as the horizon.

hover (həv′ ər). to stay in one place over a place or an object.

hypnosis (hip nō′ səs). a state that is like a deep sleep.

hypnotize (hip′ nə tīz′). to cause someone to be in a state of hypnosis.

identified flying object (IFO). (ī dent′ ə fīd flī′ ing äb′ jekt). when a UFO is later explained, it becomes an identified flying object, or IFO.

IFO. *See* identified flying object.

indentation (in den tā′ shən). a recess, or dent, in the surface of something.
interaction (int ər ak′ shən). the action of one thing with another thing.
interference (int ər fir′ əns). something that stops something else from working the way it should.
investigate (in ves′ tə gāt). to study something by close examination.
maneuver (mə nyoo′ vər). the controlled change in the path of some craft, especially an aircraft.
Mars light. the red, flashing lights on airplanes.
mathematician (math′ mə tish′ ən). an expert in mathematics.
mathematics (math ə ma′ tiks). the science of numbers and how they work.
meteor (mē′ tē ər). a piece of matter that is seen because it burns when it enters the atmosphere.
mirage (mə räzh′). a trick of the eye that causes a person to see something that is not really there.
monitor (män′ ət ər). to watch, observe, or check something for some purpose.
narrative (nar′ ət iv). something that is told.
national defense (nash′ ən əl də fens′). the military defense of a country against attack.
national security (nash′ ən əl sə kyoor′ ət ē). anything concerned with the general safety of a country.
National Weather Service. the U.S. government agency that studies and records the weather.
NL. *See* nocturnal light.
nocturnal light (näk tərn′ əl līt′). a light or lights seen at night. The observer cannot tell how far away the NL is.
North American Air Defense (NORAD). the system of defense from air attack of North America.
northern lights. *See* aurora borealis.
observer (əb zər′ vər). a person who sees something.
occult (ə kult′). having to do with things that involve the

actions or influence of the supernatural.

occupant (äk yə pənt). one who is in a certain place.

Ouija board (wē′ jə bôrd). a board that has letters and other signs and that is to receive what are supposed to be messages from spirits.

particle (pärt′ i kəl). a very small piece of something.

pattern (pat′ ərn). the similar features of something that let a person characterize that thing.

Perseid meteor shower. a group of meteors that appears every year on about August 11 in the northeastern sky.

phenomenon (fi näm′ ə nän). a rare or significant fact or event.

physical trace (fiz′ i kəl trās′). in a CE II, the evidence left by a UFO.

physicist (fiz′ ə sist). a person who is an expert in physics, which is the science that deals with matter and energy and how they interact.

prism (priz′ əm). a transparent object that can bend white light into the colors of the spectrum.

Project Blue Book. an organization set up in 1951 by the U.S. Air Force to study UFO reports. Project Blue Book ended in 1969.

Project Grudge. the Air Force project that replaced Project Sign in December 1948. The purpose of Project Grudge was to prove that UFOs did not exist.

Project Sign. a secret Air Force operation set up in 1948 to study UFO reports. Project Sign was set up because of all the public pressure for information on UFOs.

protrusion (prō trōō′ zhən). something that juts out from the surface of something.

psychologist (sī kä′ lə jəst). a person who studies the science of the mind and behavior.

radar (rā′ där). a radio device used to detect objects. Radar stands for **ra**dio **d**etecting **a**nd **r**anging.

radar-visual (RV). (rā′ där vizh′ yə wəl). the sighting of an object on a radar screen at the same time that the object is seen outdoors.

radiation (rād′ ē ā′ shən). waves of energy that are given off by something.

recur (ri kər′). to occur again after a period of time.

relativity (rel ə tiv′ ət ē). a theory of mass and energy that has to do with the speed of light and certain other laws in physics.

research (rē′ sərch). the careful study of something.

researcher (rē′ sərch ər). a person who is involved in research.

retract (ri trakt′). to draw back or in to something.

robot (rō′ bət). a machine that looks like a human being and can perform various acts.

rural (roor′ əl). relating to the country, or country life, as opposed to the city, or city life.

RV. *See* radar-visual.

satellite (sat′ əl īt). an object or vehicle made by humans to orbit the earth, the moon, or some other thing in outer space.

searchlight (sərch′ līt). a device for giving off a beam of bright light.

security clearance (si kyoor′ ət ē   klir′ əns). the authorization to see documents that the government has classified secret.

sky chart (skī′   chärt). a chart that tells the time that planets and stars will be in a certain place.

sky hook (skī′   hook). a special balloon used by the government to detect radiation.

sociologist (sō sē äl′ ə jəst). a person who studies the science of society.

spirit writing (spir′ ət   rīt′ ing). writing that a person does automatically. Spirit writing is said to be produced by the influence of spirits.

statistics (stə tis′ tiks). a branch of mathematics that deals with the collection and interpretation of large amounts of numerical information.

suggestion (səg jes′ chən). a slight hint of something.

tempo (tem′ pō). the rate of speed of something.
time exposure (tīm′ ik spō′ zhər). the exposing of film in a camera for a definite amount of time that is usually more than one half second.
transmit (tranz′ mit). to send a signal from one person or place to another.
triangular (trī ang′ gyə lər). an object that has the shape of a triangle.
twinkle (twing′ kəl). to shine with a blinking, or flickering, light.
UFO. *See* unidentified flying object.
UFO case. the result of a UFO report that has gone through the investigation of a researcher. In a UFO case, the object cannot be identified.
UFOCAT. the data bank of UFO information at the Center for UFO Studies.
UFO experience. the sighting or other contact with a UFO.
UFO report. the report of a UFO sighting to a UFO study group, police, or other organization.
undulating (ən′ jə lāt ing). rising and falling.
unidentified flying object (UFO) (ən ī dent′ ə fīd flī′ ing äb′ jekt). an object that is sighted and that even after careful research still cannot be identified.
vehicle (vē′ ik əl). any device used for carrying something.
Venus. a planet that often can be seen at night. Most nocturnal lights turn out to be sightings of Venus.
vertical (vərt′ i kəl). running up and down in relation to the horizon.
walkie-talkie (wôk′ ē tôk′ ē). a small radio that runs on batteries that can send and receive voices.
whitewash (hwīt′ wôsh). to skip over quickly or to cover something up so that the truth does not come out.
witness (wit′ nəs). a person who has personal knowledge of a fact or event.

Books

The following list represents a few of the better books available today. Other out-of-print books can be found in libraries.

Hynek, J. Allen: *The Hynek UFO Report,* New York: Dell Publishing Company, Inc., 1977.

Hynek, J. Allen: *The UFO Experience,* Chicago: Henry Regnery, 1972.

Jacobs, David: *The UFO Controversy in America,* Bloomington: Indiana University Press, 1975.

Sagan, Carl & Page, Thornton: *UFOs: A Scientific Debate,* New York: W. W. Norton & Company, 1972.

Vallee, Jacques: *Anatomy of a Phenomenon,* Chicago: Henry Regnery, 1965.

Vallee, Jacques & Vallee, Janine: *Challenge to Science: The UFO Enigma,* Chicago: Henry Regnery, 1966.

Documents

Project Magnet and Second Storey
(UFO Study for the Canadian Government)

Project Sign
(Original secret U.S. Air Force UFO Study)

Project Saucer
(U.S. Air Force Press Release Relative to Project Sign)

Robertson Report
(Panel Convened by the CIA to Study The UFO Phenomenon.)

UFOs: What to Do?
(Rand Corporation Document. A Study of the UFO Problem)

NOTE: All the above and many other scientific studies are available from: The Center for UFO Studies
1609 Sherman Avenue
Evanston, Il. USA 60201

Publications

The following list includes only publications of the United States and England. All of them have been in existence for a number of years.

The APRO Bulletin
    Aerial Phenomenon Research Organization
    3910 East Kleindale Road
    Tucson, AZ 85712

The News Bulletin and
International UFO Reporter
    Center for UFO Studies
    1609 Sherman Avenue
    Evanston, IL 60201

MUFON Bulletin
    Mutual UFO Network
    103 Oldtowne Road
    Seguin, TX 78155

UFO Investigator
National Investigators Committee on Aerial Phenomena
Suite 23
2525 University Boulevard West
Kensington, MD 20795

Flying Saucer Review
West Malling
Maidstone, England

UFO Organizations Around the World

UNITED STATES

Aerial Phenomena Research Organization (APRO)
Tucson, Arizona

Center for UFO Studies (CUFOS)
Evanston, Illinois

Civil Commission on Aerial Phenomena
Queensbridge, Ohio

Cleveland Aerial Phenomena Investigations Club
Cleveland, Ohio

Cleveland UFOlogy Project
Cleveland, Ohio

Contact International
Denville, New Jersey

Ground Saucer Watch (GSW)
Phoenix, Arizona

Mutual UFO Network (MUFON)
Seguin, Texas

National Investigations Committee on Aerial Phenomena (NICAP)
Kensington, Maryland

New England UFO Study Group
Marlborough, Massachusetts

Oak Ridge Isochronous Observation Network (ORION)
Oak Ridge, Tennessee

Odyssey Scientific Research
Baltimore, Maryland

Pennsylvania Center for UFO Studies
Pittsburgh, Pennsylvania

Project Starlight International (PSI)
Austin, Texas

Skynet
Los Angeles, California

Society for the Investigation of the Unexplained
Columbia, New Jersey

Tar Heel UFO Study Group
Winston Salem, North Carolina

Texas Scientific Research Center for UFO Studies, Inc.
McGregory, Texas

UFO Reporting Center
Seattle, Washington

UFO Research Institute
Lawndale, California

UFO Study Group of Greater St. Louis
St. Louis, Missouri

CANADA

Canadian UFO Report
Duncan, British Columbia

Manitoba Centre for UFO Studies
Winnipeg, Manitoba

New Horizons Research Foundation
Toronto, Ontario

Project S.U.M. UFO Research
St. Catharines, Ontario

UFO Canada
Chomedy Laval, Quebec

UFO Research Centre-Ontario
Toronto, Ontario

Winnipeg Independent Research Center
Winnipeg, Manitoba

MEXICO

Asociasion Investicadora del Fenomeno Ovni
Hermosillo

Centro para ia investigacion e Informacion del Fenomeno
Ovni y Parapsicologia
Colonia Cuahtemoc

DOMINICAN REPUBLIC

Grupo Observador de Fenemenos y Objetos Siderales (GOFOS)
Santiago de los Caballeros

PUERTO RICO

C.E.O.V.N.I.

S.E.F.I.N.I.

ARGENTINA

Centro de Estudios de Fenomeneos Aereos Inusuales (CEFAI)
Buenos Aires

Centro de Investigacion de Formas de Vida Estraterrestre
Buenos Aires

Circulo Argentino de Investigaciones UFOlogicas
Buenos Aires

O.N.I.F.E.
Buenos Aires

Servicio de Investigaciones UFOlogicas
Capital Federal

BRAZIL

Associacao Brasileira de Estudo das Civilizcoes Extra-terrestres
Sao Paolo

Associacao Brasillense de Pesquisa e Cultura
Brasilia

Comissae de Estudos da Vida Estraterrestre na Terre (CEVET)
Caxias do Sul

CHILE

UFO Chile
Santiago

URUGUAY

Centro de Investigacion de Objetos Voladores Inidentificados
Montevideo

ENGLAND

British UFO Documentation Centre (BUDC)
London

British UFO Research Association (BUFORA)
London

Contact (UK)
Oxford

DIGAP
South Lancaster

FAPURG
West Lancaster

Flying Saucer Review (FSR)
Maidstone

MUFORA
Manchester

Northern UFO Network (NUFON)
(various)

Nottingham UFO Investigation Society
Nottingham

PULSE
Preston

SDRUFORA
Kimberworth Park

SPRING
Sherwood

SPUR
Kettering

SUFORS
Scunthorpe

Surrey Investigation Group on Aerial Phenomena
Camberly

UFO Investigation Network
Greater Manchester

UFORA
Porthill

UFOSIS
Birmingham

WUFOS
Bromborough

NORTHERN IRELAND

UFO Research Centre
Armagh

SCOTLAND

Edinburgh University UFO Research Society
Edinburgh

AUSTRALIA

Australian Co-ordination Section — Centre for UFO Studies (ACOS)
Gosford, New South Wales

Australian Flying Saucer Research Society
Adelaide, South Australia

Tasmanian UFO Investigation Center (TUFOIC)
Hobart, Tasmania

Victoria UFO Research Society
Moorabin, Victoria

UFO Research (QLD)
Brisbane, Queensland

UFO Research (NSW)
Lane Cove, New South Wales

UFO Investigation Centre
Darwin, Northern Territory

UFO Research (FNQ)
Cairns, Queensland

UFO Research (SA)
Adelaid, South Australia

UFO Research (WA)
Rivervale, West Australia

Unidentified Phenomena Investigations Bureau
Bunbury, West Australia

NEW ZEALAND

Earth Colonisation Research Association
Paraparaumu Beach

New Zealand Scientific Space Research Group
Auckland

FRANCE

ARFA
Pessac

ASSOCIATION des Amis de Marc Thirouin (AAMT)

Centre d'Etudes and de Recherches des Phenomens Inexpliques (CERPI)
Saintes

Centre National de Recherches
Yutz

Cercle Francais de Recherches UFOlogiques (CFRU)
Forbach

Commission d'Enquetes sur les Ovnis
Valence

Commission Nationale de Recherches sur les Objets Volantes non Identifiees (CNROVNI)
Vaujours

GERS

Groupe d'Etudes Normand des Phenomenes Inconnus (GENPI)
Caen

Groupe d'Etudes Phenomenes Aerospatiaux non-Identifiee (GEPAN)
Toulouse

Groupment d'Etude des Phenomenes Aeriens
Paris

Groupement de Recherches et d'Etudes du Phenomena OVNI (GREPO)
Sorgues

Groupement de Recherches Scientifiques sur les Ovnis (GRSOVNI)
Montlucon

Groupement Troyen de Recherches sur les Ovnis (GTROVNI)
Troyes

Lumieres dan la Nuit
Haute-Loire

OURANOS
Grenoble

Societe Varoise d'Etude des Phenomenes Spatiaux (SVEPS)
Toulon

Societe Vauclusienne d'Etude Des Phenomenes Spatiaux
El Pontet

Union des Groupements Espioluguques de France et des Pays de Langue Francaise
Valence

Verification et Etude des Ovni pour Nimes et la Contree Avoisante (VERONICA)
Nimes

SPAIN

Centro de Estudios Interplanetarios (CEI)
Barcelona

Circulo de Estudios Sobre Objectos no Identificados
Valencia

PORTUGAL

Centro de Estudos Astronomicos e de Fenomenos Insolitos
Lisbon

BELGIUM

Groupemen* pour l'Etude des Sciences d'avant-garde
Brussels

Societe Beige d'Etude des Phenomenes Spatiaux (SOBEPS)
Brussels

THE NETHERLANDS

Nederlands UFO onderzaek Bureau
The Hague

NOBOVO
Uithuizermeeder

ITALY

Centro UFOlogico Nazionale
Milan

Gruppo Clypeus
Turin

Independent National Commission for the Study of Anomalous Aerial Phenomena (CNIFAA)
Bologna

La Contact International
Rome

S.H.A.D.O.
Genoa

WEST GERMANY

Centrales Enforschungsnetz Aubergewohnlicher Phanomene (CENAP) Mannheim

UFO-SIG
Berlin

YUGOSLAVIA

ODISEJA
Slovenija

DENMARK

Dansk UFO Center
Thisted

Skandinavisk UFO Information (SUFOI)
Kastrup

UFO Studiekreds
Copenhagen

FINLAND

The UFO Researchers of Finland
Turku

SWEDEN

Arbetsgruppen for UFOlogi
Sodertaije

Gotesborgs Informations Center for Oidentifierade Flygande
Foremal
Goteborg

Swedish UFO Research Center
Nassjo

100 UFO Sverige
Motala

JAPAN

CBA International
Yokohama

Japan Uchu UFO Kenkyukai
Kyushu

JSPS
Tokyo

JUFORA
Kobe

Modern Space Flight Association
Osaka

Index

Advertising plane, 47-48
Aerial Phenomena Research
    Organization (APRO), 25
Air Force, 18, 21, 22, 24, 26, 44
Airplane lights, 46-47
Airplanes
    mistaken for UFO, 40, 46
Alien, 56, 57, 58, 65
Alien case, 28
American Astronomical Society, 13
APRO. *See* Aerial Phenomena
    Research Organization
Arnold, Kenneth, 20, 21
Atmosphere, 45
Aurora borealis, 37, 38

Bible, 20
Birds, 43
Bloecher, Ted, 21
Brazil, 58
Brown, Harold D., 26

California, 53
Camera, 66
Carter, Launor, 26
Cave drawings, 20
CE I. *See* Close Encounter of the
    First Kind
CE II. *See* Close Encounter of the
    Second Kind
CE III. *See* Close Encounter of the
    Third Kind
Center for UFO Studies, 8, 21, 50,
    60, 61, 73
Central Intelligence Agency, 25
Church records, 20
CIA. *See* Central Intelligence
    Agency
Cigar-shaped object, 20
Civilian Saucer Intelligence, 25
Close encounter, 15, 28, 62
Close Encounter of the First Kind,
    15, 17, 31, 50-54, 63-64
Close Encounter of the Second
    Kind, 17, 18, 31, 54-55, 64-65
Close Encounter of the Third Kind,
    17, 18, 55-57, 65-66
Clouds
    mistaken for UFO, 49
Committee on Science and
    Astronautics, 18
Condon, Edward U., 26-27, 70
Condon Report, 27
Congress, U.S.
    hearings on UFOs, 18, 26, 27
Connecticut, 51
CSI. *See* Civilian Saucer
    Intelligence

Daylight disc, 15, 16
DD. *See* Daylight disc
Disc-shaped object, 20, 58

Electromagnetic interference, 28, 30

FAA. *See* Federal Aviation
    Agency
Far East, 20
Federal Aviation Agency, 47
Flap, 12, 13, 44
Flare, 43
Flying saucers, 13, 21
Ford, Gerald R., 26
France, 58

Gallup poll, 13
Godman Field, 21

Helicopter lights, 46-47
Helicopters
    mistaken for UFO, 47
Hynek, J. Allen, 8, 15, 25, 26
Hypnosis, 56, 57, 59

Idaho, 51

Identified flying object. *See* IFO
IFO, 37
Institute for Plasma Physics, 13
"International UFO Reporter," 36, 50
Iowa, 54
Iran, 58

Kansas, 32, 56
Kentucky, 56
Kite, 43
Korea, 60

Lenticular cloud, 49
Louisville (Kentucky), 21

Mantell, Thomas, 21
Mars lights, 40
Maxwell Air Force Base, 27
Meteor, 49
Military records, 20
Moon, 38
Mount Ranier (Washington), 20-21

National Academy of Sciences, 27
National Security Agency, 60
National Weather Service, 49
New Mexico, 55
NL. *See* Nocturnal light
Nocturnal light, 15, 16, 30, 45, 46
NORAD. *See* North American Air Defense
North American Air Defense, 49
Northern lights, 37

O'Brian, Brian, 26
Occult groups, 23
Orlansky, Jesse, 26

Parachute, 43
Pennsylvania, 52
Perseid meteor shower, 30
Physical trace, 28
Planet, 45
Police, 58

Porter, Richard, 26
Project Blue Book, 24, 27, 44
Project Grudge, 24
Project Sign, 22, 24

Quintanilla, Hector, 26

Radar, 11
Radar-Visual, 15, 16
Religious groups, 23
Report on the UFO Wave of 1947 (Bloecher), 21
Robertson, H. P., 25
Roush, J. Edward, 27
RV. *See* Radar-Visual

Sagan, Carl, 26
Saunders, David, 72-73
Science and Astronautics Committee, 27
Science fiction movies, 12
"Scientific Report on Unidentified Flying Objects," 69-70
Sky chart, 45, 46
Sky hook balloon, 22
Smithsonian Institution, 49
Space Age, 12
Spaulding, J. F., 26
Sputnik, 38
Star, 45
Stone Age, 20
Sturrock, Peter, 13

Television, 55
Test cloud, 49
Twining, Nathan F., 22
Twinkling, 46

UFO
  color of, 31, 34, 51, 52, 56, 58
  congressional hearings on, 18, 26
  description of, 11, 14-15, 31, 32, 51, 52, 53, 54, 56, 57, 58
  effect on ground, 31, 32-35, 64

    effects of, 71-72
    evidence of existence, 68-69, 71
    Gallup poll on, 13
    judging altitude, 63
    judging distance from viewer, 63
    photographs of, 66-67, 69
    reports in news media, 24, 44
    shapes of, 18, 19, 32
UFO case, 50
UFOCAT, 8, 72-73
UFO communications network, 72
UFO event, 8
UFO Experience, The (Hynek), 15
UFO report, 8-9, 10, 11, 14, 20, 21, 22, 24, 25, 31, 33, 36-37, 40, 43, 60, 68, 71, 73
    pattern to, 68-69
UFO research, 70-71
UFO study groups, 69, 71
Unidentified flying object. *See* UFO
United States government, 70-71

Venus, 22, 23, 38, 40
    mistaken for UFO, 38

Walkie-talkie, 55
Ware, Willis A., 26
Weather balloon, 49
Wright-Patterson Air Force Base, 22

Apollo Memorial Library